FINISH LINE
Reading
for the Common Core State Standards

Continental Press

Acknowledgments

Illustrations: Page 8 *sun, shovel,* 10 *tree,* 12, 16 *brush,* 34, 36 *boy,* 39 *trash,* 42, 61, 78, 94, 105, 113, 123, 126, 132, 147, 153, 156, 159, 160, 174, 178, 183, 193, 215: Laurie Conley; Page 16 *shell:* Eric Hammond; Page 16 *bee,* 31, 33, 36 *girl,* 37, 48, 120: Jane Yamada; Page 40 *ship:* Michael Fink; Page 59: Kristi Valiant; Page 100: David Schimmell; Page 196: Margaret Lindmark; Page 207: Kristi Gerner

Photographs: Page 24: www.istockphoto.com/MariaPavlova; Page 26: Image used under Creative Commons from Brunel University; Page 40: Jeremy Woodhouse; Page 45: www.istockphoto.com/tbradford; Page 51: www.shutterstock.com, Olga Bogatyrenko; Page 55: www.photos.com; Page 64 *dairy farm:* PhotoLink; Page 64 *vegetable farm:* www.photos.com; Page 69: PhotoLink; Page 83: PhotoLink; Page 86: www.istockphoto.com/adlifemarketing; Page 90: www.airscooter.com; Page 98: www.istockphoto.com/wolv; Page 109: www.istockphoto.com/jrphoto6; Page 116: Cynthia Moss. © 2000–2003 African Elephant Conservation Trust. All rights reserved. Page 130: www.istockphoto.com/David Philips; Page 133: www.wikipedia.org; Page 139: www.istockphoto.com/ArtisticCaptures; Page 145: *Freedom Ship.* Copyright © 2002–2003, Freedom Ship International, Inc. (FSI). *Freedom Ship* is a Trademark of FSI. All Rights Reserved. Page 149 *kangaroo:* www.istockphoto.com/Jeremy Edwards; Page 149 *cassowary:* www.istockphoto.com/CraigRJD; Page 166: Image used under Creative Commons from Aaron Silvers; Page 182: Library of Congress, Prints and Photographs Division, LC-DIG-pga-04179; Page 188: www.istockphoto.com/Figure8Photos; Page 190: www.istockphoto.com/MaszaS; Page 203: www.istockphoto.com/bonniej; Page 205: Kim Steele; Page 209 *pokatok goal:* www.istockphoto.com/oralleff; Page 209 *pokatok court:* www.istockphoto.com/bbourdages

ISBN 978-0-8454-6910-1

Copyright © 2011 The Continental Press, Inc.

No part of this publication may be reproduced in any form or by any means, electronic, mechanical, photocopying, recording, or otherwise, without the prior written permission of the publisher. All rights reserved. Printed in the United States of America.

Table of Contents

Introduction 4

Unit 1: Vocabulary Development 5

RF.1.2, RF.1.3	Lesson 1	Sounds of Words	6
RI.1.4, RF.1.4, L.1.4	Lesson 2	Word Meanings	17
RL.1.4, L.1.5	Lesson 3	Word Relationships	29
	Review	Vocabulary Development	38

Unit 2: Key Ideas and Details 43

RL.1.1, RI.1.1	Lesson 4	Understanding a Text	44
RL.1.2, RI.1.2	Lesson 5	Main Idea and Summaries	54
RL.1.3	Lesson 6	Literary Elements	67
RI.1.3	Lesson 7	Analyzing Events and Concepts	81
	Review	Key Ideas and Details	93

Unit 3: Craft and Structure 103

RL.1.5	Lesson 8	Types of Literature	104
RL.1.6	Lesson 9	Point of View	119
RI.1.5, RI.1.6	Lesson 10	Text Features	128
	Review	Craft and Structure	144

Unit 4: Integration of Knowledge and Ideas 151

RL.1.7, RI.1.7	Lesson 11	Visual Literacy	152
RI.1.8	Lesson 12	Identifying Connections	164
RL.1.9, RI.1.9	Lesson 13	Comparing and Contrasting	173
	Review	Integration of Knowledge and Ideas ..	192

Practice Test 199

Glossary 219

Welcome to Finish Line Reading for the Common Core State Standards

This book will help you become a good reader. It will also help you to get ready for reading tests.

The lessons in this book follow the Common Core State Standards for English Language Arts and Literacy in History, Social Studies, Science, and Technical Subjects. The Common Core State Standards (CCSS) build on the education standards developed by the states.

In the lessons of this book, you will read stories and informational text. Then you will answer multiple-choice and writing questions about them. The lessons in this book are in three parts:

- The first part talks about the reading skill you are going to study and explains what it is and how you use it.

- The second part is called Guided Practice. You will get more than just practice here; you will get help. You will read a story, poem, or nonfiction article. Then you will answer questions about it. After each question, the correct answer will be explained to you.

- The third part is called Test Yourself. You will read a passage. Then you will answer questions on your own.

There is a Review Lesson at the end of each unit. You will be able to show what you learned. There is also a Practice Test at the end of the book.

Now you are ready to begin using this book. Good Luck!

Vocabulary Development

You are learning to read. And you are learning to write. You will find a lot of new words. Use clues to help you find a word's meaning. You need to know how to use different words. These lessons will help you become a better reader and writer.

- **Lesson 1** shows you how to use phonics. You will look at parts of words. You will learn what letters sound like. Then you will be able to sound out words.

- **In Lesson 2,** you will find the meanings of words. You do not always know what a word means. You can use clues in the sentence. They help you find the meaning of the word. You will also learn about prefixes and suffixes. These change the meaning of a word.

- **In Lesson 3,** you will look at words that describe. You will look at playful language. And you will look at words that can be grouped together.

Sounds of Words

Lesson 1

RF.1.2, RF.1.3

All words are made up of letters. A letter can be a **consonant.** Or a letter can be a **vowel.** Consonants and vowels make up all the sounds of words.

Long and Short Vowels

The vowel letters are **a, e, i, o,** and **u.** Vowels can have more than one sound. They may be **short** vowels. Or they may be **long** vowels.

Short	Long
cat	tape
wet	Pete
hid	hide
hot	rope
rub	cube

Do you see a pattern? Look at the words with short vowels. There is usually a consonant sound after the vowel. Look at the words with long vowels. There is usually a silent **e** after the consonant sound.

can   cane

Sometimes the letter **y** is a vowel, too. It might sound like a long **e**. It might sound like a long **i**.

| lady | sky |

Say these words to yourself. Listen to the long vowel sounds.

below	dry	notice
cable	higher	player
date	kind	super
decide	maker	tune

Consonant Sounds

All the other letters are consonants. Listen for consonants in words. You can hear them at the beginning of words. You can hear them in the middle of words. You can hear them at the end of words.

Look at this picture. Say the word out loud. Listen for the consonant sound at the beginning.

The word has the sound /s/. It starts with **s.** The word is sun.

Look at this picture. Say the word out loud. Listen for the consonant sound at the end.

The word has the sound /n/. It ends with **n.** The word is wagon.

Look at this picture. Say the word out loud. Listen for the consonant sound in the middle.

The word has the sound /v/ in the middle. It has a **v** in the middle. The word is shovel.

Guided Practice

Say each word to yourself. The underlined part of the first word stands for a vowel sound. Find the word that has the same vowel sound. Circle the letter for this word.

r<u>i</u>ng

- **A** tide
- **B** finger
- **C** afraid
- **D** taxi

 Listen for the short **i** sound in <u>ring</u>. The word <u>finger</u> has the same short **i** sound. Choice B is correct.

fl<u>a</u>ke

- **A** march
- **B** heat
- **C** sand
- **D** gray

 Listen for the long **a** sound in <u>flake</u>. The word <u>gray</u> has the same sound. The correct answer is choice D.

Read each question. Look at the picture. Say the word to yourself. Circle the letter of the best answer.

Which word has the same ending sound?

   A leaf
   B house
   C man
   D head

   The picture is a crown. The ending sound in crown is /n/. Say each choice. The only one that ends with /n/ is man. Choice C is correct.

Which word has the same beginning sound?

   A train
   B town
   C there
   D tank

   This picture is a tree. The beginning sound is /tr/. The word train has the same beginning sound. Choice A is correct.

Vowel Teams and Consonant Teams

Two vowels can work as a team. They can stand for one sound. They are called **vowel digraphs.** The sound is usually the long vowel sound of the first letter.

ai	r**ai**n	ea	m**ea**t	oa	b**oa**t
ay	p**ay**	ee	b**ee**tle		

Two consonants can work as a team. They are called **consonant digraphs.** They make a new sound. Consonant teams can be at the beginning of a word. They can be at the end of a word, too.

ch	**ch**air	th	ba**th**
sh	pu**sh**	wh	**wh**eel

Guided Practice

Look at each picture. Circle the word with the same sound.

Which has the same ending sound?

A dock
B chain
C hatch
D cane

The picture is a watch. Choices B and C have the **ch** consonant team, too. The sound is at the beginning of choice B. It is at the end of choice C. Choice C is correct.

Which has the same vowel team sound?

A nose
B cheer
C name
D pail

The picture is a nail. <u>Nail</u> has the vowel team **ai**. The word <u>pail</u> has the same vowel team. Choice D is correct.

UNIT 1
Vocabulary Development

Which has the same beginning sound?

    A math

    B ten

    C thin

    D track

 The picture shows a thumb. The beginning sound of <u>thumb</u> is /th/. <u>Thin</u> has the /th/ sound in the beginning. <u>Math</u> has the /th/ sound at the end. Choice C is correct.

Which has the same vowel team sound?

    A coat

    B sand

    C stood

    D across

 The picture is soap. <u>Soap</u> has the **oa** vowel team. <u>Coat</u> has the same vowel team. Choice A is correct.

Test Yourself

Say each word to yourself. The underlined part of the first word stands for a vowel sound. Find the word that has the same vowel sound. Circle the letter for this word.

1 d<u>i</u>me

   A bit

   B hide

   C hair

   D dish

2 m<u>e</u>ss

   A meet

   B scene

   C neat

   D sent

3 d<u>a</u>nger

   A chief

   B dart

   C baker

   D action

Look at the picture. Circle the word with the same sound.

4 Which word has the same middle sound?

- A mother
- B high
- C leather
- D water

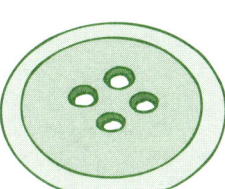

5 Which word has the same ending sound?

- A cream
- B dish
- C rug
- D tune

6 Which word has the same beginning sound?

- A help
- B pond
- C leave
- D ripe

7 Which word has the same beginning sound?

  A wash

  B shed

  C there

  D star

8 Which word has the same vowel team sound?

  A bat

  B treat

  C day

  D pan

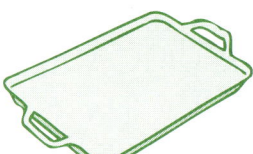

9 Which word has the same ending sound?

  A sharp

  B brain

  C bus

  D fish

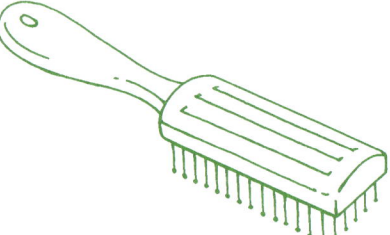

10 Which word has the same vowel team sound?

  A weed

  B bed

  C well

  D sand

Lesson 2: Word Meanings

RI.1.4, RF.1.4, L.1.4

You are learning a lot of new words. Read a new word. Do you know what it means? Look for **context clues.** These clues are in the sentence. They help you find the meaning of a word.

Context Clues

You use context clues. You might not even know it. You try to figure out words from how they are used. Look at part of Robert Louis Stevenson's poem, "At the Seaside." Do you know what the underlined word means?

> When I was down beside the sea
> A wooden spade they gave to me
> To dig the sandy shore.

You probably do not know what a spade is. Look at the rest of the poem. The speaker is at the beach. Look at what he does with the spade. He digs in the sand. You can guess that a spade is a shovel.

In the poem, we found context clues from the other words. This is called **association.** There are other ways to find context clues. Look at the chart below.

Type of Clue	Unknown Word	Clue
Similar Words (synonyms)	The **famous** actor also has a well-known sister.	The word well-known means the same thing as famous.
Contrast	The outside of the house was **shabby.** But inside it was very clean.	The word shabby is contrasted with "very clean." You know that shabby must mean dirty.
Description	Our **neighbor** is the person who lives next door to us.	The word neighbor is described in the sentence.
Series	The book had photos, drawings, and **diagrams.**	You may not know exactly what diagrams are. But you can guess they are a type of picture.
Cause and Effect	The twins are **identical.** So no one can tell them apart.	You can guess that identical means they look the same.

UNIT 1
Vocabulary Development

Guided Practice

Write the word that would best fit the sentence.

Ladybugs give off a bad _____ to keep enemies away. *(smell, color, light)*

> Did you guess smell? Use **cause and effect**. You may not know what enemies are. But ladybugs want to keep them away. So they are bad. If something smells bad, you would not go near it. Ladybugs keep their enemies away. They give off a bad smell.

In chilly weather, ladybugs like to _____ in sunny areas. *(swim, rest, jump)*

> Did you guess rest? You may not know what chilly means. Chilly is another word for cold or cool. You can guess that. Use a **contrast** clue. Contrast chilly and sunny. The ladybugs try to stay warm. They sit in sunny places.

Multiple-Meaning Words

Sometimes words have more than one meaning. This can be tricky. Sometimes you will think of one meaning. Look at the context. It might show you a different meaning. You have to think about all the meanings. Then you can know which one is right. Look at the example below.

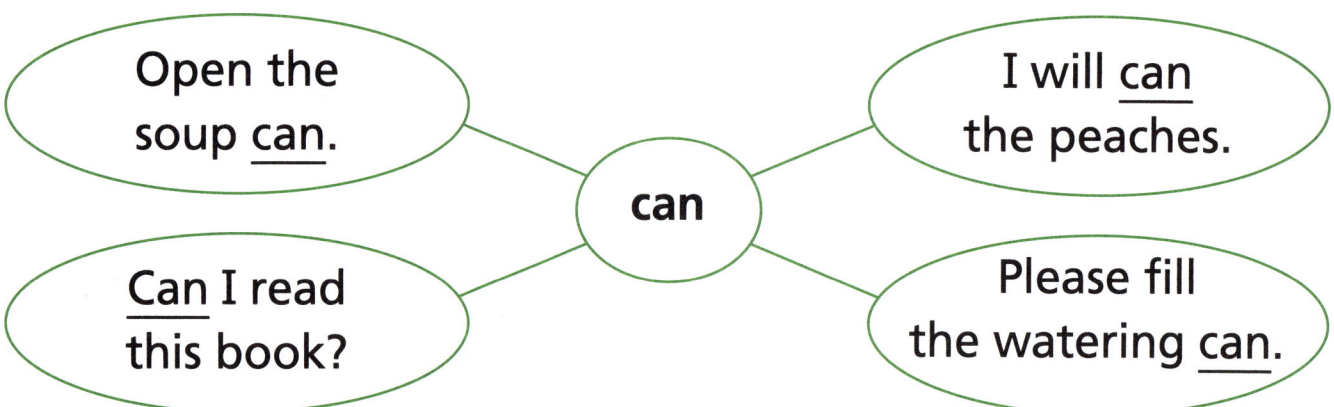

There are many words with multiple meanings. Can you think of different meanings for these words?

ball   bat   bit   trip   pet   jam   pen   cut

Guided Practice

Read each sentence. Find the sentence that uses the word exactly the same way it is used in the main sentence.

I will be right **back.**

  A Can you scratch my back?

  B I must back up the car.

  C When will you be back?

  D My dad hurt his back.

  Choices A and D are a part of the body. Choice B is a direction. Choice C shows that someone is returning. Choice C is correct.

Please **hand** me a spoon.

  A Give a hand for the next singer!

  B You must hand me the book.

  C I have five fingers on my hand.

  D I need a hand to help lift this box.

  Choice A means to clap for someone. Choice C is a part of the body. Choice D means help. Choice B means to give something to someone. Choice B is the correct answer.

Prefixes, Suffixes, and Roots

Words can have prefixes and suffixes. A **prefix** is added to the beginning of a word. It changes the meaning of a word. A **suffix** is added to the end of the word. Look at the word unhelpful. It has a prefix and a suffix. Un- is the prefix. It means "not." The suffix -ful means "full of." Unhelpful means "not full of help."

Look at the charts below. You will see some common prefixes and suffixes.

Prefix Chart

Prefix	Meaning	Root for New Word	New Word
re-	again, back	turn	return
un-	not	fair	unfair

Suffix Chart

Suffix	Meaning	Root for New Word	New Word
-ed	past tense verb	hop	hopped
-ful	full of	wonder	wonderful
-ing	present participle verb	run	running
-ly	having qualities	friend	friendly
-s, -es	more than one	boy, box	boys, boxes

Guided Practice

Read each sentence. Then tell whether the underlined word has a prefix or a suffix. Circle prefix or suffix.

Laura had to <u>un</u>tie her shoelace.   prefix   suffix

Hyo <u>asked</u> for another cookie.   prefix   suffix

The new kitten was very <u>playful</u>.   prefix   suffix

Did you get them all right? The first sentence has a prefix. The other sentences have suffixes.

What words do you know that start with a prefix?
What words do you know that end with a suffix?
Make a list.

_____

_____

_____

These are some words with prefixes: **un**happy, **re**do, **un**hurt, **re**grow. These are some words with suffixes: glad**ly**, bed**s**, care**ful**, beach**es**, jump**ing**. Did you have any of these words on your list?

UNIT 1
Vocabulary Development
23

Test Yourself

Read the paragraph. Then answer the questions.

Ann and her family were going on a long journey. They left early in the morning. They walked to the train station. Then they got on the train. The train went from the city to the country. The ride was bumpy. Ann could feel the whole train tremble as it moved along. She looked out the window. The towns and villages were flying past.

1 Read these two sentences.

   The ride was bumpy. Ann could feel the whole train tremble as it moved along.

   Use cause and effect context clues. What does tremble mean?

   A shake

   B move

   C jump

   D hold

2 Which sentence uses the word <u>long</u> as it is used in the first sentence of the paragraph?

　A How <u>long</u> until we eat?

　B That is a <u>long</u> piece of string.

　C She has very <u>long</u> hair.

　D This is a <u>long</u> movie.

3 Read this sentence.

　The towns and <u>villages</u> were flying past.

　Use a similar word for a context clue. Tell what <u>villages</u> means.

_____

_____

_____

_____

4 Which word means almost the same as <u>journey</u>?

　A morning

　B trip

　C station

　D city

Read the story. Then answer the questions.

World's Fastest Man

What is faster than a lightning bolt? Maybe Usain Bolt. Usain Bolt is the world's fastest man.

Bolt grew up in Jamaica. It is a small island. He loved to play sports. He could run very fast. He decided to just practice running.

He worked very hard. His coach helped him. In 2008, he went to the Olympics. The Olympics are games for the best <u>athletes</u>. People from different countries come. They play many sports. They all want to be the best. They all want to win a gold medal. Bolt was <u>hopeful</u>. He wanted to win.

The 100-meter race is short. You have to start fast. And you have to stay fast. The winner is named "World's Fastest Man."

Bolt ran faster than everyone else. There was no one near him. He even slowed down a bit at the end. He still won! He set a <u>record</u>, too. He ran the race in 9.69 seconds. And his shoe was <u>untied</u>.

Bolt is not finished. He is still running. And he is having fun, too. Just look at his smile.

5 Read this sentence from the story.

The Olympics are games for the best athletes.

Use context clues. What does athletes mean?

A people who run

B people who win

C people who play sports

D people who are from Jamaica

6 What does untied mean?

A tied again

B not tied

C tied tightly

D tied twice

7 Read these sentences from the story.

He still won! He set a record, too.

Use context clues. Tell what a record is.

_____

_____

_____

_____

8 What does hopeful mean?

   A no hope

   B full of hope

   C to hope again

   D in the same way as hope

Lesson 3: Word Relationships

RL.1.4, L.1.5

We use words everyday. Some words describe things. You might say, "The bed was soft." <u>Soft</u> tells how the bed felt. Sometimes we use words **figuratively** (FIG•yur•uh•tiv•lee). This means we are playful with language. Playful language helps describe things. It helps people make a picture in their minds. You could say, "The bed was like a cloud." This also describes the bed as soft.

Figurative Language

Figurative language makes you think about something in a different way. You think about how the words make you feel.

You may compare two things that are not alike. You can use the words <u>like</u> or <u>as</u>. This is called a **simile** [SIM•uh•lee].

She is as mean as a bear.

You may **exaggerate** [EGG•zah•juh•rayt]. This means you stretch the truth.

My backpack weighs a ton.

You may compare two unlike things. You do not use the words <u>like</u> or <u>as</u>. This is called a **metaphor** [MET•uh•for].

The road was an ice rink.

Guided Practice

Answer the questions.

Look at these sentences. Which one uses language playfully?

- **A** I put the cupcakes in the oven.
- **B** Mom and I baked a million cupcakes.
- **C** My favorite cupcakes are chocolate.
- **D** We put sprinkles in the icing.

Did you guess choice B? Of course, they did not actually make a million cupcakes. This is an exaggeration. It helps you know that they made a lot of cupcakes. The writer is using language playfully.

Look at these sentences. Which one uses language playfully?

A I was dreaming of the beach.

B I was playing in the blue water.

C Then I heard a loud noise.

D My alarm clock was a truck horn.

Choice D is the correct answer. It compares an alarm clock and a truck horn. It does not use the words like or as. It is a metaphor. It helps you hear how loud the alarm seems.

Look at these sentences. Which one uses language playfully?

A The seat was as cold as ice.

B I wrapped up in a blanket.

C The blanket was warm and fuzzy.

D I sipped my hot chocolate.

Did you guess choice A? It uses playful language. It compares the seat to ice. It uses the word as. This sentence is a simile. It helps you feel how cold the seat was.

Similar Words

There are many words to describe. These words are called **adjectives.** You can describe people. You can describe places, too. And you can describe things. Sometimes words mean almost the same thing. Similar words are called **synonyms.**

Say you wanted to describe a hot day. You already used the word hot. You need another word. These are other words that mean almost the same thing:

burning   warm   spicy

The words burning and warm could fit. The word spicy does not. Think about burning and warm. Burning probably makes you think of something really hot. Something that is warm is not as hot. So burning is the best choice.

Guided Practice

Answer the questions.

Which word *best* fits this sentence?
She wanted to ____ her new bike.

   A drive

   B ride

   C sail

   D move

 All the answer choices are close. There is one that fits best. The correct answer is choice B. *Drive, sail,* and *move* all tell about going someplace. But *ride* tells about going someplace on a bike.

Which word *best* fits this sentence?
Troy had a ____ toy truck.

   A little

   B young

   C short

   D few

 All these words talk about something that is small. Only one word works for a toy. The toy truck was little. Choice A is correct.

Words in Categories

You can put words in groups. Groups that have something in common are **categories.** Look at these words:

    cat   bear   lion   fish

What makes these words go together? They all name animals.

Guided Practice

Read each group of words. Pick the choice that tells why the words go together.

Read these words.

   shoe   hat   coat

A These words name things to put on.

B These words name things to do.

C These words name places to go.

D These words name foods to eat.

Think about shoes, a hat, and a coat. What do you do with these things? You wear them. They are things you put on. The correct choice is A.

Read these words.

dolls   blocks   balls

A These words name people.

B These words name animals.

C These words name colors.

D These words name toys.

Think about these things. They are not people or animals. They are not color names. They are toys that you play with. Choice D is correct.

Test Yourself

Answer the questions.

1. Look at these sentences. Which one uses language playfully?

   A I jumped into the big pool.

   B I made a huge splash.

   C I was a fish swimming in the water.

   D I wore my new red swimsuit.

2. Look at these sentences. Which one uses language playfully?

   A Sam hit the ball hard.

   B Sam ran as fast as lightning.

   C The ball flew through the air.

   D Sam had hit a home run.

3. Look at these sentences. Which one uses language playfully?

   A The scouts hiked a thousand miles.

   B Amir's legs were very tired.

   C He had to carry a backpack and water.

   D The trail was beside a stream.

4 Which word *best* fits this sentence?

Laila ____ a picture with her new crayons.

A painted

B did

C colored

D wrote

5 Which word *best* fits this sentence?

Eric licked the ____ icing off the cookie.

A nice

B kind

C gentle

D sweet

REVIEW

Unit 1 — Vocabulary Development

Read each word. Look at the underlined part of the first word. It stands for a vowel sound. Find the word that has the same vowel sound. Circle the letter for that word.

1 gl<u>a</u>ss
- **A** hair
- **B** marry
- **C** late
- **D** bay

2 m<u>i</u>nd
- **A** pink
- **B** lip
- **C** file
- **D** him

3 r<u>u</u>g

  A four

  B huge

  C rib

  D cuff

Look at the picture. Circle the word with the same sound.

4 Which word has the same beginning sound?

  A paw

  B water

  C throw

  D mow

5 Which word has the same ending sound?

  A wash

  B chase

  C fast

  D class

UNIT 1
Vocabulary Development

6 Which word has the same beginning sound?

- **A** push
- **B** seed
- **C** shoe
- **D** tip

7 Which word has the same vowel team sound?

- **A** bake
- **B** pest
- **C** roar
- **D** beach

Read the paragraph. Then answer the questions.

Rhinos

Grown rhinos do not have any enemies. Rhinos are just too tough. They have thick skin and long horns. Baby rhinos are not as lucky. Fast lions chase them. Grown rhinos take care of the babies. They make a circle around the babies. Then, the rhinos point their horns out. Lions will not go in a circle of rhino horns. Most lions run away quickly.

8 Which sentence uses point the same way it is used in the paragraph?

　A What is the point of this book?

　B Do not point your finger at me.

　C The hat has a point on top.

　D Each answer is worth one point.

9 Which word means the same as tough?

　A slow

　B sad

　C strong

　D old

10 What does quickly mean?

　A quick again

　B not quick

　C full of quick

　D in a quick way

Answer the questions.

11 Look at these sentences. Which one uses language playfully?

　A This is my favorite movie.

　B I have watched it a million times.

　C This character looks like my aunt.

　D The ending is very funny.

12 Look at these sentences. Which one uses language playfully?

　A The paper was as white as snow.

　B I used bright red paint.

　C I painted a big apple.

　D My mom hung up the picture.

13 Which word *best* fits this sentence?

The sun is very ____ today.

　A bright

　B light

　C shiny

　D smart

UNIT 1
Vocabulary Development

Unit 2: Key Ideas and Details

You will read many different things. Some books have stories and poems in them. Some books tell about history. Some tell you how to make something. You read to find out more. When you read, there are big ideas. These are called **main ideas.** There are also smaller ideas. These are called **details.** Details tell more about the main ideas. Everything you read has main ideas and details.

- **Lesson 4** tells you about details. You will learn how to find details. This will help you remember what a story is about.

- **In Lesson 5**, you will find the main ideas. You will also tell about what you have read.

- **Lesson 6** will help you learn about what makes up stories and plays. You will find details about people in stories. You will think about what happens in stories. And you will think about where and when a story takes place.

- **Lesson 7** helps you find main ideas and details, too. You will read nonfiction. You will learn about events. And you will make guesses about what will happen.

LESSON 4: Understanding a Text

RL.1.1, RI.1.1

Vocabulary
- mangrove
- office
- president
- stories
- swamp

The things you read have **details.** Details give more information. They tell about characters. They tell about places. Details tell more about what is happening. They make reading more fun! Think about the details when you read. You do not want to miss what the author is telling you.

Guided Practice

Read the passage. Then answer the questions.

Mangrove Swamps

A swamp is a wet place. It has many plants and animals. Sometimes trees grow there. Their roots may be under the water most of the time. Swamps are home to frogs, snakes, and birds. But what is a mangrove swamp? How is it different from other swamps?

A mangrove is a special kind of tree. Most trees need fresh water. They cannot grow in salt water. That is why trees do not often grow too close to the ocean. A mangrove tree is different. It can grow in salt water. A mangrove

swamp
land that is wet and often covered in water

mangrove
a tree that grows in some swamps

swamp has hundreds of these trees. They grow near each other. Most mangrove swamps are found where fresh water from a river meets salt water.

Mangrove swamps are important. Many kinds of animals lay eggs there. Animals have babies there. The swamps help keep the area safe. They keep dirt from washing away. People need to take better care of mangrove swamps before they are all gone.

What is a mangrove?

   A a type of animal

   B a type of water

   C a type of egg

   D a type of tree

> Look at the text. Paragraph 2 says that a mangrove is a special kind of tree. Choices A, B, and C are incorrect. Choice D is the correct answer.

Why is a mangrove tree different from other trees?

  A It has roots.
  B It grows in salt water.
  C It does not need water.
  D It does not have leaves.

This detail is in paragraph 2. A mangrove tree has roots and leaves. This is like other trees. It does need water. This is also like other trees. Most trees only grow in fresh water. But mangrove trees can grow in salt water. The correct answer is choice B.

How can people help the mangrove swamps?

  A They can cut down trees.
  B They can take the animals as pets.
  C They can take care of them.
  D They can make more swamps.

Choice C is the correct answer. Look at the last paragraph. It tells you that people need to take care of the swamps. They should not cut down trees. They should not take the animals for pets. The passage does not say that people need to make more swamps.

Why are mangrove swamps important?

_____

_____

_____

_____

_____

 Think about what you read. The last paragraph tells you this detail. Here is a sample answer:

> Animals live in the swamps. Animals have babies there. These animals might not live anywhere else. The swamps also help keep the area safe. They keep dirt from washing away. This helps the plants to grow.

Read the story. Then answer the questions.

Birthday Surprise

Jason likes to ride bike. He asked for a new bike for his birthday. His old bike was too small.

Jason's birthday came. He was so excited for his new bike.

"Happy Birthday," Mom and Dad said. They handed Jason a small box. The box was too small to hold a bike.

Jason tried to smile. "Thanks," he said.

He slowly opened the box. Jason found a letter in the box. The letter said, "Look behind the house." Jason ran to the back of the house. There he saw a brand new green bike! It was just the bike he wanted.

"Surprise!" cried Mom and Dad.

"This is the best gift!" Jason said as he jumped on his new bike.

What did Jason want for his birthday?

- **A** a dog
- **B** a ball
- **C** a wagon
- **D** a bike

The correct answer is choice D. The first paragraph gives the answer. It says he asked for a new bike for his birthday. The story does not talk about a dog, ball, or wagon.

Who gave Jason the birthday surprise?

- **A** his friends
- **B** his mom and dad
- **C** his brother and sister
- **D** his grandmother and grandfather

Look back at the story. Jason's mom and dad gave him a small box. But inside was a letter telling him how to find the bike. The bike was a gift from his mom and dad. Choice B is correct.

How did Jason feel when he got the box?

_____

_____

 You must make a guess to answer this question. Look at what the story says. Use that to make a good guess. Here is a sample answer:

> Jason felt sad. He had hoped for a bike for his birthday. He knew the bike would not fit in the box. He tried to smile. But he felt let down.

What color was Jason's birthday surprise?

  A blue
  B green
  C red
  D yellow

 Look at the end of the story for this detail. The story says there was a "brand new green bike." The correct answer is choice B.

Test Yourself

Read the passage. Then answer the questions.

The White House

Did you know that you own one of the biggest houses around? The White House is one of the biggest houses in the United States. The White House is where the president of the United States lives and works. It has rooms for his family. And it has the president's offices. These are the rooms where the president and his helpers work. That is why it is so big.

Most houses have six or seven rooms. The White House has 132 rooms. Most houses have two or three stories. The White House has six stories! There is a movie theater in the White House. There is a bowling alley and a swimming pool, too.

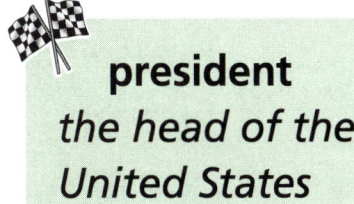
president
the head of the United States

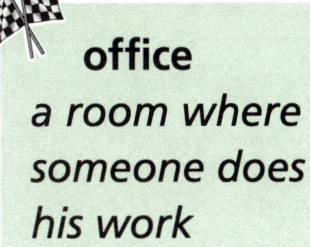
office
a room where someone does his work

stories
the floors in a building

The president does not own the White House. He only lives there while he is president. When another president is chosen, the old president has to move out. Then the new president moves in. Only one president did not live in the White House. That was George Washington. He was the first president of the United States.

The people of the United States own the White House. That is why the White House is sometimes called "The People's House."

1 Who lives in the White House?

   A George Washington

   B the president of the United States

   C the people of the United States

   D the president's helpers

2 How many rooms are in the White House?

   A 132

   B 125

   C 7

   D 6

3 Which of these is *not* in the White House?

  A a movie theater

  B a swimming pool

  C a bowling alley

  D an ice skating rink

4 Who does the White House belong to?

  _____

  _____

  _____

5 Why do you think George Washington did not live in the White House?

  _____

  _____

  _____

  _____

Lesson 5: Main Idea and Summaries

RL.1.2, RI.1.2

Vocabulary
harvest
passages
products
pyramids
treasures

Tell a friend about a book you read. You try to tell her in a few sentences. You probably give her the **main idea.** The main idea is what the story is about. It is important for you to find the main idea. This is a key reading skill.

Guided Practice

Read the passage. Then answer the questions.

Egypt's Pyramids

Egypt is a country in north Africa. People first lived in Egypt long, long ago. They built special buildings. The buildings were called pyramids.

The pyramids of Egypt were made of stone blocks. The stone blocks were huge! Each pyramid had four walls. Each wall was a triangle. The pyramids were very tall.

It took many people to build the pyramids. They did not have machines. They had to use their hands. They used animals, too. They had

pyramids
large buildings with four walls that are shaped like triangles

to move the big stones. They had to put them in place. It took them a long time to build each pyramid.

The people built the pyramids for the kings of Egypt. The kings wanted to be buried in the pyramids. There were many rooms inside. There were secret passages. There were traps. The kings had many treasures. They wanted to be buried with their treasures.

passages
hallways

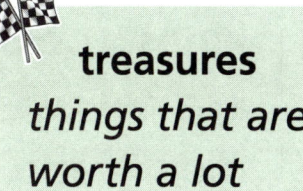

treasures
things that are worth a lot

There are a lot of pyramids in Egypt. So far, people have discovered 138 pyramids. People come from all over the world. They want to see these amazing buildings.

What is this passage *mainly* about?

A Egypt

B kings

C treasures

D pyramids

The passage talks about Egypt. It talks about kings, too. And it talks about treasures. But those are not what it is mostly about. The passage is mostly about pyramids. Choice D is correct.

Which sentence *best* shows the main idea of paragraph 4?

A There were many rooms inside.

B They wanted to be buried with their treasures.

C The people built the pyramids for the kings of Egypt.

D There were secret passages.

Most times, there is one sentence that tells the main idea of a paragraph. This is the **topic sentence**. In this paragraph, it is the first one. The other sentences tell details. Choice C is the correct answer.

What is the main idea of paragraph 3?

_____

_____

_____

Think about what the details tell you. This will help you find the main idea. Here is a sample answer:

> The main idea of paragraph 3 is that many people helped build the pyramids. The details tell what they did. They tell why it took so many people.

Which of these details should *not* be in a summary of the passage?

A There were traps in the pyramids.
B The pyramids were built for the kings.
C The kings wanted to be buried in pyramids.
D The pyramids were very big.

A **summary** tells the main ideas. It tells the most important details. Choices B, C, and D are all important details. A summary does not need to tell about the traps. Choice A is correct.

Write a summary of the passage.

_____
_____
_____
_____
_____
_____
_____
_____

 Think about the main idea of each paragraph. Here is a sample answer:

> The pyramids are huge buildings in Egypt. They were built a long time ago. Many people helped to build them. The pyramids have four sides. The sides are shaped like triangles. The kings of Egypt were buried in pyramids. You can still go to see the pyramids today.

A Bell for the Cat
an Aesop's fable

Once there was a group of mice. They had a problem. The cat would sneak up on them. He would surprise them. Then he would eat them. The mice were very scared of the cat.

One day, the mice got together. They wanted to make a plan. They needed to stay safe from the cat. But what could they do it?

"I have an idea," one mouse said. "The cat is sneaky. We do not know where he is. We should put a bell on the cat. Then we will hear the bell ring. We will know where the cat is. Then we can run away and hide."

"That is a good plan!" cried the other mice. They clapped and clapped.

Then Old Mouse got up. "It is a good plan," he said. "Now, who is brave? Who will put the bell on the cat?"

The mice all got very quiet. They looked at each other. Then the mice all walked away. No one would put the bell on the cat.

So the cat could still sneak up on the mice. And the mice were still scared of the cat.

What is the mice's problem?

A They need a bell.

B They are scared of the cat.

C They are hungry.

D They need a new home.

This question asks for an important detail. Look at the first paragraph. The cat sneaks up on the mice. Then the cat eats the mice. The mice are scared of the cat. The correct answer is choice B.

What was the mouse's plan?

_____

_____

_____

_____

This is another detail in the story. Here is a sample answer:

The mouse said they should put a bell on the cat. Then the cat could not sneak up on the mice. The bell would ring. They would know where the cat was.

What is the moral of this story?

 The main idea of a text is sometimes called its **theme.** The theme is what a story is about. In a fable, the theme is often a lesson. It is called a moral. Here is a sample answer:

It is easier to talk about a plan than to do it.

Read this poem. Then answer the questions.

At the Zoo
by William Makepeace Thackeray

1. First I saw the white bear, then I saw the black;
2. Then I saw the camel with a hump upon his back;
3. Then I saw the grey wolf, with mutton[1] in his maw[2];
4. Then I saw the wombat waddle in the straw;
5. Then I saw the elephant a-waving of his trunk;
6. Then I saw the monkeys—mercy, how unpleasantly they smelt!

[1]**mutton:** type of meat
[2]**maw:** animal's mouth

What is the main idea of this poem?

   A The poet smells something bad.

   B The poet is looking at animals at the zoo.

   C The poet is lost at the zoo.

   D The poet does not like going to the zoo.

> The poet talks about different animals he sees. He is at the zoo. He sees bears, a camel, a wolf, a wombat, an elephant, and monkeys. The correct answer is choice B.

What is the wolf doing in the poem?

   A sleeping

   B running

   C growling

   D eating

> Look at line 3. It says the wolf has "mutton in his maw." You might not know two of these words. The meanings are below the poem. Mutton is a type of meat. Maw is an animal's mouth. The wolf has meat in his mouth. He is eating. Choice D is correct.

What detail does the poet tell about the monkeys?

_____

_____

 Read the last line of the poem. Here is a sample answer:

The poet says that the monkeys do not smell good.

UNIT 2
Key Ideas and Details

Test Yourself

Read the passage. Then answer the questions.

All Kinds of Farms

There are a lot of farms all over the world. Not all farms are the same. Some grow vegetables. Some have animals. And some even grow fish!

There are many cows on a dairy farm. A dairy farm makes milk. It might make other dairy products, like cheese. The farmer takes care of the cows. He feeds them. He makes sure they have water. And he keeps them healthy. Every day, the farmer milks the cows. He might milk them by hand. Or he might use a machine. A machine helps him milk many cows at the same time. Then the farmer sells the milk.

products
things that are made

A vegetable farm grows many kinds of vegetables. Vegetables grow best in different seasons. The farmer harvests peas and radishes in the spring. She picks corn and tomatoes in the summer. She gathers broccoli and celery in the fall. The farmer might sell the vegetables to people. She might sell them to restaurants. Many people like to eat fresh vegetables!

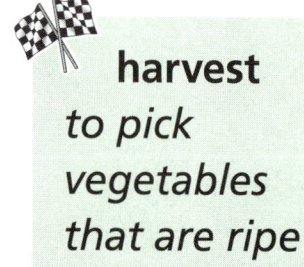

harvest
to pick vegetables that are ripe

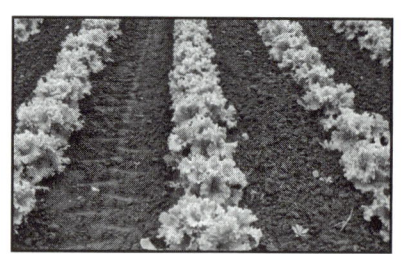

A fish farm raises fish. The farmers get the fish when they are very little. They put the fish in ponds. They feed the fish. They keep the water clean. Then the fish grow. Finally the fish get big. Then the farmers take them out of the ponds. They sell the fish for food.

Think about the food you like to eat. It probably came from some kind of farm!

1 What is the main idea of this passage?
   A Dairy farms have cows.
   B Vegetables are grown at different times.
   C There are many kinds of farms.
   D People eat food from farms.

2 What is the main idea of paragraph 3?
   A Vegetables grow in different seasons.
   B A vegetable farm grows many kinds of vegetables.
   C The farmer sells the vegetables.
   D People like to eat vegetables.

3 What does a dairy farm make?

    A broccoli

    B fish

    C tomatoes

    D milk

4 Write a sentence that tells the main idea of paragraph 4.

_____

_____

5 Write a summary of the passage.

_____

_____

_____

_____

_____

_____

Lesson 6

Literary Elements

RL.1.3

Vocabulary
cast
chuckled
frightened
outwit
reel

Some stories are fiction. This means they are made-up. They are not true. Stories are all different. But they have parts that are the same. A story has **characters.** Characters are the actors in the story. A story has a **plot.** The plot is what happens. There is often a problem. The plot tells how the characters solve the problem. A story has a **setting.** The setting is when the story takes place. It is also where the story takes place. All these things make a good story.

Analyzing a Character

Characters make the story real. The author tells how the characters talk, look, and act. You can learn about a character in different ways:

- What the character does
- What the character says
- What others say about the character
- What the author says about the character

UNDERSTANDING A CHARACTER

UNIT 2
Key Ideas and Details

Guided Practice

Read the story. Then answer the questions.

Going Fishing
by Juan Martinez

"Wake up, sleepyhead," Grandpa said.

I rolled over. I was going to go back to sleep. Then I remembered! Today was the day!

I jumped out of bed. Grandpa already had everything in the car. He was making breakfast.

"Are you ready to learn to fish?" Grandpa asked.

"Yes!" I said. Grandpa loved to fish. He had promised to teach me when I was old enough. Finally the day had arrived. I even had my own fishing rod. It was smaller than Grandpa's. It was the right size for me.

I ate in the car while Grandpa drove. We went to Aunt Eva's house. She was ready and waiting for us. The three of us drove to the lake together.

"Stormy Lake is my favorite place to fish," said Aunt Eva. "You will really like it here, Juan."

"I can't wait," I told her excitedly.

Finally, we got there. It was still early in the morning. But I was wide awake. Grandpa showed me how to put a worm on my hook. He showed me how to cast the line. Soon I got the hang of it.

cast
to throw a fishing line into the water

Suddenly, I felt a tug on my line! I called for Grandpa. He helped me reel in my very first fish. I held it up. Grandpa took a picture of me with my fish. I had a big smile on my face.

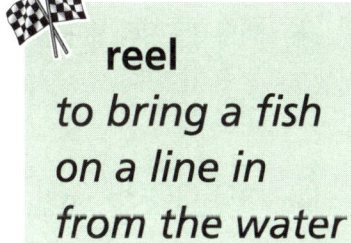

reel
to bring a fish on a line in from the water

"You can show this picture to your mom," Grandpa said. "Then she can see your first fish."

Later, Grandpa caught a fish. Then Aunt Eva caught a huge fish. That night we ate fresh fish for dinner.

Who is *not* a character in this story?

  A Juan

  B Aunt Eva

  C Grandpa

  D Juan's mom

> The correct answer is choice D. Juan is telling the story. Both Grandpa and Aunt Eva are in the story. Grandpa talks about Juan's mom. But she is not in the story.

What do we know about Juan by what he does?

  A He is scared to go fishing.

  B He is excited to go fishing.

  C He does not like Aunt Eva.

  D He does not like worms.

> Juan jumps out of bed. He says that he cannot wait. He listens to what Grandpa tells him about fishing. He is excited to go fishing. Choice B is correct.

What is the big event in this story?

　　A Juan and Grandpa visit Aunt Eva.

　　B Grandpa shows Juan how to cast a line.

　　C Juan catches his first fish.

　　D Aunt Eva catches a huge fish.

> What is this story mostly about? This is Juan's first fishing trip. He catches his first fish. That is the big event. Choice C is the correct answer.

Describe the two settings of the story.

_____

_____

_____

> The setting is where the story takes place. This can include the time of day. It can also include the location. A story can have more than one setting. Here is a sample answer:

　　　　The story starts at Juan's house early in the morning. The rest of the story takes place at Stormy Lake. This is where Juan, Grandpa, and Aunt Eva go fishing.

Elements of Drama

A **play** is a story that is acted out. A play is broken into **acts** and **scenes.**

The list of the **characters** in a play is called the **cast.** The characters act out the play's action. The **setting** is when and where the play takes place.

The **dialogue** is the words the characters say. These words come after the character's name.

Stage directions tell actors how to move. They tell actors where to go on stage. The directions can also tell them how to say their lines.

Look at this play. It is the same story as on page 59.

Guided Practice

Read the play. Then answer the questions.

A Bell for the Cat
a one-scene play

Cast of Characters:
Mouse #1
Mouse #2
Old Mouse
Other Mice

SCENE 1

A mouse home in the wall of a house. A door in the wall shows the people's home, where the Cat lives. A group of mice are talking loudly.

MOUSE #1: Ok, ok! Everyone quiet, please!

The mice stop talking. They look at Mouse #1.

MOUSE #1: We have a problem. The Cat is too sneaky. We go out to find food. But the Cat finds us. We can't hear him coming. So we can't get away.

Other mice nod.

MOUSE #1: We need a plan. We need to do something. Does anyone have an idea?

Other mice look at each other. They shake their heads. Some of them shrug.

MOUSE #2 *(raises his hand and speaks quietly):* I have an idea.

MOUSE #1 *(speaks to Mouse #2):* Come up. Tell us your plan.

MOUSE #2 *(walks to front of group. He looks at the other mice):* We need to know where the Cat is. Then we can get away from him. We need to be able to hear him coming.

MOUSE #1: But the Cat does not make noise. He is too quiet.

MOUSE #2 *(holds up bell):* We should put a bell on the Cat. When the Cat moves, the bell will ring. Then we will know where he is. We can run away.

OTHER MICE: Good plan! Good idea! Let's do it!

All the mice nod and smile. They clap their hands.

OLD MOUSE *(stands up and speaks loudly):* That is a very good plan.

All the mice look at Old Mouse. They listen to him quietly.

OLD MOUSE: Now, who is brave? Who will put the bell on the Cat?

The mice look at each other. Some of them look at the floor. No one says anything.

OLD MOUSE *(looking around the group):* You are all too scared. No one will put the bell on the Cat. So the plan will not work. It is easier to think of a plan than to do it.

All the mice walk away sadly.

Which of these is an example of dialogue spoken by Mouse #1?

- A That is a very good plan.
- B Ok, ok! Everyone quiet, please!
- C *(speaks to Mouse #2)*
- D MOUSE #1

> The italic type is used for directions (choice C). The regular type shows what is spoken (choices A and B). CAPITALS show the name of the character who is talking (choice D). Old Mouse speaks the lines in choice A. Mouse #1 speaks the lines in choice B. So choice B is correct.

What is an example of a prop used in this play?

_____

_____

> A **prop** is an object that can be moved easily. Actors use the props in the play. Scenery is the background. It is bigger. It is harder to move. Here is a sample answer:

One prop used in the play is the bell. Mouse #2 holds up the bell. He shows it to the other mice.

Read these lines from the play.

> MOUSE #2 *(walks to front of group. He looks at the other mice):* We need to know where the Cat is. Then we can get away from him. We need to be able to hear him coming.

What do the stage directions in italic tell you?

A where Mouse #2 moves

B how Mouse #2 talks

C what Mouse #2 says

D what Mouse #2 is wearing

> The directions tell the actor what he should do. The correct answer is choice A. Mouse #2 was with the group of mice. Then he walks to the front of the group. He looks at the mice when he says these lines.

Test Yourself

Read the story. Then answer the questions.

Why Cats Don't Wash Their Hands Before They Eat

a story from Africa

A long, long time ago, cats did not wash their hands or faces. Then one day, something happened to change that. A big cat was walking through the jungle. She was strong and beautiful. Cat saw a little bird. So she caught the bird. She wanted to eat it for lunch. Bird was frightened. He did not know what to do. He was too small to get away from Cat. He did not have sharp teeth. He did not have claws. His only chance was to outwit Cat.

"Oh, Cat," Bird said. "You are so strong and beautiful. You must be very important. But I am surprised that you have such bad manners."

"What do you mean?" asked Cat. She held Bird up and looked at him.

"Well," said Bird, "everyone knows that the most important animals always wash their hands before they eat."

"Is that so?" said Cat. "I am the most important animal of all. I will do it, too."

frightened *scared*

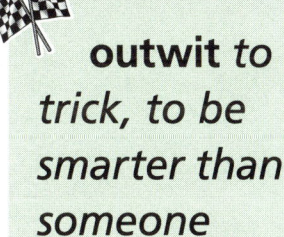

outwit *to trick, to be smarter than someone*

Cat put Bird down on the ground. Then she started to lick her paws. And she washed her face. Bird flew quickly to a high branch in a tree. There he chuckled at Cat. He sang a song because he was happy.

chuckled
laughed

Cat was upset. She did not like to be tricked by Bird. From that day on, she only washed after she finished eating.

That is why you see cats washing themselves after they eat. They never wash before they eat. They learned their lesson.

1 Which word *best* describes Cat?

A kind

B proud

C scared

D smart

2 What is the setting of the story?

    A jungle

    B house

    C tree

    D meadow

3 Cat was interested in Bird because she was ____.

    A nosy

    B friendly

    C worried

    D hungry

4 How did Bird get away from Cat?

_____

_____

_____

_____

5 What is the main problem in this story?

_____

_____

_____

_____

6 How do you think Cat feels at the end of the story?

_____

_____

_____

_____

Lesson 7

Analyzing Events and Concepts

RI.1.3

Vocabulary
collect
controls
engine
honor
traffic

Ideas, events, and people are often connected. People think of ideas. Then they do things a certain way. People can make events happen. Events can also make people act a certain way.

Here is an example. There were not many people living in California. An event caused people to move there. Somebody found gold in California. Other people wanted to find gold, too. This caused many people to leave their homes. They moved to California to look for gold.

Think about different things when you read. Think about the order things happen. Ask yourself, "Why did that happen?" Then you can find the cause of an event. Ask, "What happened because of this?" This helps you find the effect.

Clue words can help you.

Clue words for cause:	Clue words for effect:
if	then
because	so
since	as a result

UNIT 2
Key Ideas and Details

Look for connections when you read. This will help you understand what you are reading.

Guided Practice

Read the story. Then answer the questions.

A Penny Saved
by Neil Smith

Look at the coins in your piggy bank. Do you have one that is a different color than the other coins. It is a penny! The penny is worth one cent.

The penny was first made in 1793. The penny has changed over the years. Today, it has a picture of Abraham Lincoln on it. He was the 16th president. People wanted to honor Abraham Lincoln. They said he had been a great president. So, they put his face on the penny.

At one time, you could buy a piece of candy for just one penny. A stamp for a letter cost only two pennies. Today, you cannot buy anything for just one penny. So why do we still have pennies? Pennies are used to make change. You buy a pack of gum for 98 cents. You pay with a $1 bill. Then you will get two pennies as change.

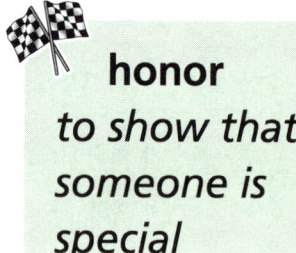

honor
to show that someone is special

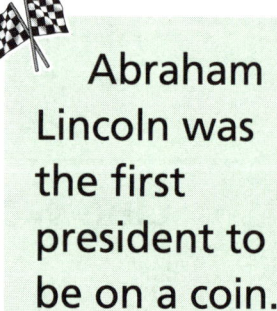

Abraham Lincoln was the first president to be on a coin.

UNIT 2
Key Ideas and Details

Some people want to get rid of pennies. They say we do not need them. They want to change prices. So we would not use the penny.

Other people like pennies. Some people collect them. Some people try to find old pennies. Old pennies can be worth a lot of money. Other people save pennies. After a while, the pennies you save will add up to a dollar.

What do you think should happen to the penny?

collect
to gather a group of something

Why is Abraham Lincoln's face on the penny?

   A because he was a president

   B because the penny is a different color

   C because he made the penny

   D because people wanted to honor him

> This question makes you think about cause and effect. The effect is that Abraham Lincoln is on the penny. What caused this? People wanted to honor him. Choice D is correct. Abraham Lincoln was president. But that was not the only reason he is on the penny.

People want to get rid of pennies. What would be an effect of not having pennies?

A Prices would change.

B People could not find old pennies.

C You could not buy gum.

D Abraham Lincoln would not be president.

People would still be able to find old pennies. You could still buy gum. Abraham Lincoln was president a long time ago. That would not change. Prices would have to change. There could not be pennies in prices. The correct answer is choice A.

According to the story, what event happened *first*?

_____

_____

_____

Think about the story. Think about what had to happen before everything else. Here is a sample answer:

> The first thing that had to happen was that pennies were made. If pennies were never made, nothing else would have happened.

UNIT 2
Key Ideas and Details

Why do some people collect old pennies?

___

___

___

___

 This question asks you to draw a **conclusion**. You must think about what the story said. The answer may not be written out in the story. You have to put ideas together. Here is a sample answer:

> Old pennies are worth a lot of money. They are worth more than one cent. People like to collect things that are worth money. It makes them more special.

Read the recipe. Then answer the questions.

Mini Pizzas

6 plain bagels, cut in half

16 ounces tomato sauce

3 cups shredded mozzarella cheese

Pizza toppings, such as green pepper, onion, or pepperoni

1. Preheat the oven to 325°F.
2. Spread tomato sauce on the bagel halves.
3. Put the shredded cheese on top of the tomato sauce.
4. Add your favorite toppings.
5. Put the bagel halves on a baking sheet.
6. Bake the bagel pizzas in the oven. Leave them in for 5 to 8 minutes. Watch for the cheese to get bubbly. Then the pizzas are done.
7. Let the pizzas cool for a few minutes. Then eat!

Which of these steps do you do *first*?

    A Spread tomato sauce on the bagel halves.

    B Preheat the oven to 325°F.

    C Add toppings.

    D Bake the bagel pizzas in the oven.

> You must follow steps in order when you make food. If you do not, your food might not taste very good. Look at the recipe carefully. Look for the first step. First you preheat the oven. Choice B is correct.

What step do you do right *after* you spread the tomato sauce on the bagels?

    A Preheat the oven to 325°F.

    B Put the bagel halves on a baking sheet.

    C Add toppings.

    D Put the shredded cheese on top.

> Follow the steps in order. Step 2 says to spread the tomato sauce on the bagels. Step 3 tells you to put cheese on top. Choice D is the correct answer.

What might happen if you did not do step 1?

_____

_____

_____

_____

> ✓ This question asks you to make a good guess, or a **prediction.** You need to bake the bagels. You do not want them to be cold. Here is a sample answer:

    The first step is to heat the oven. If you don't do this, the oven won't get hot. You will want to bake the bagels. But the oven will be cold.

Test Yourself

Read the passage. Then answer the questions.

Up, Up, and Away!
by Olivia Ramirez

Imagine flying through the air. Not in a plane. Not in a hot air balloon. But in your own air scooter! Someday people may be using air scooters to go places.

One person can sit in an air scooter. He uses the hand controls to move it. He can go straight up in the air. He can go left and right. He can come straight back down to the ground. There are no foot controls in the air scooter. The person uses just his hands. So a person who cannot walk can still fly!

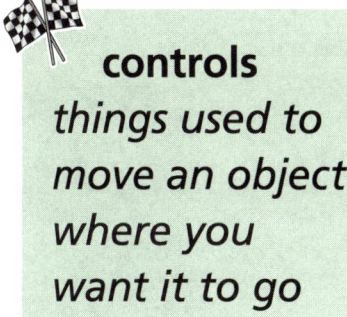
controls *things used to move an object where you want it to go*

An air scooter cannot fly very high. It cannot fly as high as airplanes. But it can fly over the roofs of houses. The air scooter has a special engine. It is not like the engine in other things. It is only for the air scooter. The air scooter has blades on top. The blades go around in circles. The blades go very fast. The blades help the scooter go up and down.

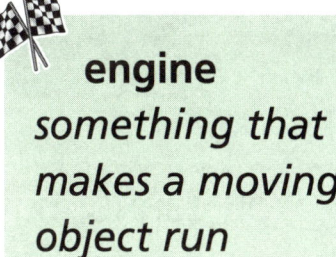
engine *something that makes a moving object run*

Wouldn't it be fun to fly an air scooter? It would be faster than driving in a car. You would not have to stay on a road. You would not get stuck in traffic. The air scooter is not very big. You could park it in your driveway.

traffic
cars and trucks on roads

You cannot buy an air scooter yet. The people who make them are still working on them. They want to make sure there are no problems. They want to make sure air scooters are safe. But maybe someday you will have an air scooter!

1 You cannot buy an air scooter yet because _____.

   A they fly over roofs of houses

   B they might not be safe yet

   C they are too small

   D they have special engines

UNIT 2
Key Ideas and Details

2 What does a person use to tell the air scooter where to go?

   A blades

   B engines

   C foot controls

   D hand controls

3 Why does an air scooter have a special engine?

   _____

   _____

   _____

   _____

4 Think of a person who cannot walk. Why can that person still use an air scooter?

   _____

   _____

   _____

   _____

5 Why do you think an air scooter would be better than a car?

_____

_____

_____

_____

REVIEW

Key Ideas and Details

Unit 2

Vocabulary
porridge
stilts
triangular

porridge
oatmeal

Read the story. Then answer the questions.

The Magic Porridge Pot

Long ago, a little girl lived alone with her mother. They were very poor. One day, they ran out of food.

The little girl went to the forest. She looked for apples to eat. She looked and looked. But she could not find any apples. The little girl sat down on a log. She began to cry. An old woman came up to her.

"What is the matter, little girl?" the woman asked.

"My mother and I do not have any food," the little girl said.

The old woman smiled. She reached into her bag. Then she pulled out an old pot.

"This is a magic porridge pot. Watch and see what it can do," the woman said.

The old woman spoke to the pot. "Cook, little pot, cook," she said. Then the pot cooked good, sweet porridge. The old woman said, "Stop, little pot." And it stopped cooking.

The little girl ran home with the pot. Her mother was very happy. Now they would always have food.

One day, the little girl was away. Her mother was hungry.

"Cook, little pot, cook," she said. The pot cooked. The mother ate until she was full. But the pot kept on cooking.

The mother wanted the pot to stop cooking. But she did not know the words.

"Don't cook anymore!" she yelled. But the pot went on cooking. The porridge rose over the edge of the pot. It spilled out on the floor.

"No more porridge!" cried the mother. But the pot went on cooking. The whole house was soon full of porridge. It ran out the door. It ran down the street. It ran into other houses.

Finally the little girl came home. "Stop, little pot!" she yelled. And it stopped cooking. But the whole village was full of porridge. The people had to eat their way back to their homes.

1 What was the little girl looking for in the forest?

   A porridge

   B a cooking pot

   C apples

   D the old woman

2 Why does the pot not stop cooking?

   A The little girl is away.

   B The mother does not know the right words.

   C The mother is mean to the little girl.

   D The little girl is very hungry.

3 What was magical about the pot?

   A It could cook any kind of food.

   B It was very old.

   C It could make porridge.

   D It could talk.

4 Which of these words describes the old woman in the forest?

   A kind

   B mean

   C funny

   D angry

5 How did the little girl *most likely* feel when she got the magic pot?

   A upset

   B scared

   C sad

   D excited

6 Which of these details does *not* belong in a summary of the story?

   A The little girl is poor.

   B The little girl sat on a log.

   C An old woman gave the little girl a magic pot.

   D The mother did not know the words to stop the pot.

7 What is the setting of this story?

   A a village long ago

   B a big city long ago

   C a make-believe land in the future

   D a magic forest in the future

8 What is the lesson in this story?

   A Always share with others.

   B Listen to people older than you.

   C Do not take things from strangers.

   D Too much of a good thing can be bad.

Read the passage. Then answer the questions.

Campfires

Have you ever gone camping? Then you probably sat around a campfire at night. You might have told stories. And you might have roasted marshmallows. Campfires can be a lot of fun. But you have to be safe, too.

First, you need to know how to make a campfire. Start with very thin, dry twigs. These are called tinder. They will catch fire right away. Next, pile on some twigs that are a little larger. They can be about as thick as your finger. These are called kindling. Finally, have some bigger branches and logs. You will put them on when the fire is burning well.

Do not forget to be safe! Always have an adult with you. Get the area ready before you start the fire. Clear a space about ten feet wide. Get rid of any leaves and trash. Keep a bucket of water near. The fire may get too big. Do not get too close to the fire. And never leave the fire without someone watching it.

Remember these tips. Then your campfire will be great!

9 Kindling should be about as thick as your ____.

A finger

B arm

C leg

D waist

10 What should you do *first?*

　　A Clear the area.

　　B Put big logs on the fire.

　　C Put tinder on the fire.

　　D Watch the fire carefully.

11 What is the main idea of this passage?

　　A how to have a fun camping trip

　　B the best places to go camping

　　C campfire tips and safety

　　D ways to help adults

12 Which is *not* a way to be safe around a campfire?

　　A Keep a bucket of water near.

　　B Clear the space around the fire.

　　C Have an adult with you.

　　D Sit very close to the fire.

13 Tell three steps to build a campfire.

　　1. _____

　　2. _____

　　3. _____

Read the passage. Then answer the questions.

Walking Tall

Have you ever wished you were taller? You can make your own stilts! They will make you taller! Plus they are a lot of fun.

1. Supplies you will need:
   - large matching juice cans, unopened (64 ounces)
   - can opener with triangular end
   - long pieces of rope
   - scissors
   - colored tape
   - paints and paintbrushes
2. Have an adult help you with this step. Use the can opener. Punch two holes in each can. The holes should be right across from each other.
3. Drain the juice. You can put it in a container to save. Rinse the cans. Let them dry.
4. Take the labels off the cans.

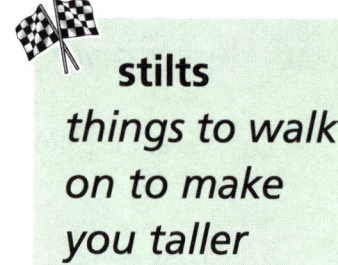
stilts
things to walk on to make you taller

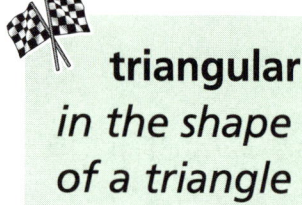
triangular
in the shape of a triangle

5. Have an adult help you with this step. Cut two pieces of rope. Measure each piece. Hold one end at your waist. Let the rope down to the ground. Step on the rope with both feet. Then bring it back up to your waist. Cut the piece a little longer than this length.

6. Put each piece of rope through the holes in the cans. Use one piece of rope for each can.

7. Tie the two ends of the rope together. These are your handles.

8. You might want to put tape around the knots. This will help them stay tied.

9. Use the paints. Decorate your stilts. Let the paint dry.

10. Put one foot on each can. Hold the handles in your hands. Now walk tall!

14 What is the *first* step you should take to make the stilts?

A Drain the juice out of the cans.

B Get your supplies.

C Cut the rope.

D Paint the cans.

15 What is the main point of step 5?

    A to give a list of supplies

    B to tell how to decorate your stilts

    C to tell what to do with the juice

    D to tell how to measure the rope

16 Why should an adult help you with steps 2 and 5?

_____

_____

_____

_____

17 Why do you need matching juice cans?

_____

_____

_____

_____

UNIT 2 — Key Ideas and Details

Unit 3: Craft and Structure

Think of a writer as a builder. He uses words to build. A writer builds a poem with words and lines. She builds a story with words and sentences. He builds nonfiction with words and sentences, too.

- **In Lesson 8,** you will learn about different types of writing. You will learn about fiction, or made-up stories. And you will learn about nonfiction. Nonfiction is stories that are true.

- **Lesson 9** tells you about point of view. You will find out who is telling the story. Point of view shapes what you read.

- **Lesson 10** shows you text features in nonfiction. You will learn about different features. You will learn how to use them to understand what you read.

Lesson 8

Types of Literature

RL.1.5

Vocabulary
argument
extinct
nutrition
observe

There are many kinds of books. Some books are fiction. **Fiction** is made-up stories. Sometimes the stories might seem real. But they are not true. They are just for fun. Some books are **nonfiction.** These books have true information. They might tell you about real people. Or they might tell you how to make something.

Both kinds of books help you learn new things. You need to be able to tell what kind of book you are reading. You need to know if it is true.

Books with Stories

You learned about stories in Lesson 6. Stories have **characters.** Stories have a **plot,** or problem. And stories have a **setting.** The characters work to fix the problem. Stories have a beginning, middle, and end. You usually meet the characters in the beginning. You learn about the setting. You begin to learn about the problem. The middle tells what happens. It tells how the characters try to solve the problem. The end tells how the problem is solved.

Guided Practice

Read the story. Then answer the questions.

The Goose That Laid Golden Eggs
an adaptation

One day a farmer's wife found a strange egg. It was in a goose's nest. The egg was very heavy. And it was yellow.

"Oh my, this is a golden egg!" she cried.

She checked the nest each morning. There was always another golden egg. The farmer and his wife became rich. But they wanted even more.

"That goose must be full of gold!" the farmer's wife said.

They made up a plan. They wanted to get all the goose's gold. That night, the farmer and his wife cut open the goose. But there was no gold inside. Now they could not get any more gold. They had killed the goose that laid the golden eggs.

Where might you find this story?

- A in an animal magazine
- B in a dictionary
- C in a book of fables
- D in a history book

The correct answer is choice C. This is a fable. It tells a story that is not true. It teaches a lesson. An animal magazine and a history book tell about true things. A dictionary gives words and their meanings.

What lesson does this story teach?

- A Do not try to get too much.
- B Be kind to all animals.
- C Friends are a good thing.
- D Never have a goose for a pet.

A fable teaches a lesson. The farmer and his wife got a golden egg every morning. They wanted even more. So they killed the goose to get all the gold. But there was no gold inside the goose. They tried to get too much. So they will have nothing. Choice A is correct.

Tell what happens in the beginning, middle, and end of the story.

Beginning _____

_____

Middle _____

_____

End _____

_____

> ✓ Think about each part of the story. Here is a sample answer:

   Beginning   The farmer's wife finds a golden egg.

   Middle   The farmer and his wife get a golden egg every morning. They become rich. They want more gold. They decide to cut open the goose to get the gold.

   End   The farmer and his wife find out there is no gold inside the goose. Now they do not have any gold at all.

Books with Information

Some books tell about real things. They might tell about real people. They might tell about real things that happened. Or they might tell you about how to do something. There are many things these books could tell about. These books are different than books with stories. They do not have characters. They do not have a plot. And they do not have a setting. There is no problem to solve. You read these books to learn things.

Guided Practice

Read the passage. Then answer the questions.

Polar Bears and Goose Eggs

Polar bears live near the North Pole. The ground at the North Pole is ice. It is cold there all the time. Polar bears like the cold weather. They use the ice to walk across the water. They travel far to look for food.

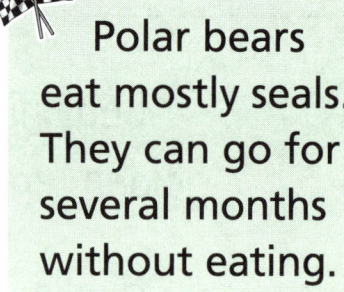
Polar bears eat mostly seals. They can go for several months without eating.

The North Pole is getting warmer. This means that the ice is melting. Polar bears cannot travel as far. So they cannot find as much food. People are worried about polar bears. They are afraid that polar bears will become extinct.

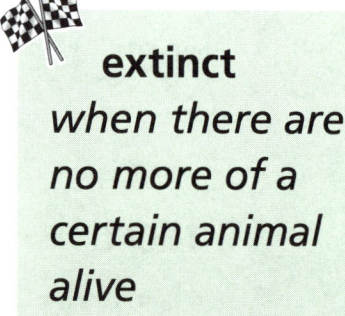
extinct
when there are no more of a certain animal alive

Polar bears are trying a new food. They eat goose eggs! There are many snow geese where polar bears live. They lay eggs. Sometimes polar bears come and eat the eggs. The eggs are good for the polar bears. They get nutrition that they need.

nutrition
things that animals and people need to stay healthy

Polar bears help the snow geese, too. There are a lot of snow geese. Sometimes there are too many snow geese. There is not enough food for all of them. Polar bears eat some of the eggs. There are still many snow geese. But now there is enough food for them all.

Where might you find this passage?

A in a book of fairy tales

B in a magazine about animals

C in a magazine of poems

D in a dictionary

This passage is nonfiction. It tells about something true. So it is not a fairy tale or a poem. A dictionary tells words and their meanings. This passage talks about polar bears and goose eggs. It could be in a magazine about animals. Choice B is correct.

How do you know this is not a made-up story?

_____

_____

_____

Think about what is in a story. Here is a sample answer:

> A story has characters. It has a plot. And it has a setting. This does not have characters, a plot, or a setting. It tells about polar bears. It gives information.

UNIT 3
Craft and Structure

Think about the story, "The Goose That Laid Golden Eggs." Think about the passage "Polar Bears and Goose Eggs." Tell one thing that is the same. Tell two things that are different.

Same _____

_____

Different _____

_____

 Look back at the story you read. Think about the passage, too. Here is a sample answer:

Same   Both talk about how goose eggs help people or animals.

Different   The story teaches a lesson. The passage does not teach a lesson.
The story is not true. The passage is true.

Test Yourself

Read the story. Then answer the questions.

The Elephant and the Monkey
a story from India

Elephant and Monkey were friends. They played in the jungle together. Monkey liked to swing from tree branches. Elephant liked to make a path in the jungle. He used his strong trunk. One day, Monkey and Elephant had an argument.

"I am the strongest animal," said Elephant. He wrapped his trunk around a small tree. He pulled the tree out the ground.

"I am the quickest animal," said Monkey. He ran up a big tree. He swung on the branches. He hung from his tail.

"It is better to be strong than quick," said Elephant.

"No, it is better to be quick than strong," said Monkey.

The two could not decide who was right. They decided to ask Owl. Owl was very wise. He would know the answer.

"Is it better to be strong? Or is it better to be quick?" they asked Owl.

argument
not thinking the same about something

Owl said, "Go to the tall tree with the golden fruit. Pick a piece of fruit. Then bring it back to me."

Monkey and Elephant left to do what Owl said. Soon they came to a river. The tree was on the other side. The river was deep. The water was moving fast.

"I cannot cross the river," Monkey said.

"I am strong," said Elephant. "I can cross it. You must ride on my back. I will carry you."

So Elephant crossed the river. Monkey rode safely on his back.

They looked up at the fruit on the tree. It was very high. Elephant tried to pull the tree out of the ground. He could not do it. He tried to reach the fruit with his trunk. It was too high.

"I can get it," Monkey said. He ran up the tree. He picked a piece of fruit. Then he ran back down the tree.

Elephant and Monkey went back to Owl. They gave him the fruit.

"Owl, now tell us," they said, "is it better to be strong? Or is it better to be quick?"

Owl said, "Which one of you brought me this fruit?"

"I crossed the river to get to the tree," said Elephant.

"I climbed the tree to pick the fruit," said Monkey.

"Then you brought it together," said Owl.

Elephant and Monkey thought about it. They could not have picked the fruit alone. They needed each other. Elephant and Monkey stopped fighting. They went back to playing.

1 Where would you find this story?

   A in a dictionary

   B in a book of tales

   C in a book of poems

   D in a magazine about trees

2 Who is *not* a character in the story?

   A Owl

   B Monkey

   C Elephant

   D Bear

3 How do you know this is fiction?

_____

_____

_____

_____

4 What happens in the beginning of the story?

   A Monkey and Elephant have an argument.

   B Monkey and Elephant cross the river.

   C Monkey and Elephant bring the fruit to Owl.

   D Monkey and Elephant talk to Owl.

5 Tell what happens at the end of the story.

_____

_____

_____

_____

Read the passage. Then answer the questions.

Cynthia Moss

Over 30 years ago, Cynthia Moss went to Africa. She wanted to see the elephants. She was just going to stay for a few weeks. But she is still there today. Cynthia stayed because she wanted to learn about elephants. She wanted to help elephants, too.

Cynthia learned a lot about elephants. She learned that they live in big families. She learned that older mother elephants are the bosses of the families. She also learned how to tell one elephant from another. She can tell elephants apart by their ears. Elephants' ears have marks on them. No two elephants' ears are the same.

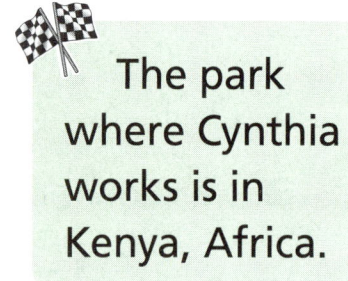

The park where Cynthia works is in Kenya, Africa.

Cynthia works in a park for elephants. Other people work there, too. They try to keep the elephants safe. They observe the elephants. They want to find out more about them.

There are many elephants in the park. They all have names. Cynthia knows all of the elephants' names. Cynthia tells other people about the elephants. She wants other people to know about the elephants. Then other people can help them, too.

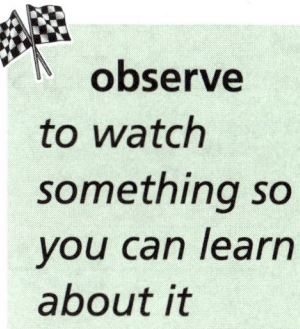

observe
to watch something so you can learn about it

6 Should this passage be in a book of stories? Or should it be in a book of information? Tell how you know.

_____

_____

_____

_____

7 Think about the story "The Elephant and the Monkey." Think about the passage "Cynthia Moss." Tell something that is the same about them.

_____

_____

_____

_____

8 Think about the story and the passage. What is the main thing that is different about them?

_____

_____

_____

_____

Lesson 9

Point of View

RL.1.6

Vocabulary
castles
confused
roam

All writing has a **point of view.** Authors write about things they know. You may read a story about a dog. The author has a pet dog. He thinks dogs are the best pets. That is his point of view. You might read another story about a dog. A dog bit the author. She is scared of dogs. That is her point of view.

Each story feels different to the reader. Point of view changes how it feels. *Who* is telling a story? *Why* is the author writing? *Who* is the author? *How* does the author want me to feel? Ask *who, why,* and *how* when you read.

The person who tells a story is a **narrator.** Sometimes the story is told by one character. The person uses the word *I* or *you.* Some stories are told by more than one character. Or, they are told by someone who is outside the story. These stories use the words *he, she,* and *they.*

UNIT 3
Craft and Structure

Poems have a point of view, too. The **speaker** is the person telling a poem. This person might be a character. Or she might be someone outside the poem.

Guided Practice

Read the story. Then answer the questions.

Forgotten Birthday

Something seemed wrong that morning. Alexa was sure that her family would wish her a happy birthday. Her mom made her breakfast. She did not say anything. Her dad drove her to school. He did not say anything. Her brother walked her to her classroom. He did not say anything either. Had everyone forgotten?

At school, Alexa's friends acted strange. Even her best friend Ellen would not talk to her. Alexa was feeling sad. This was the worst birthday ever! Everyone had forgotten.

Alexa walked home from school slowly. She was not excited for her birthday dinner. She was not excited for birthday presents. Everyone had forgotten.

When she got home, the house was dark. Alexa was confused. She was a little scared, too. Where was everyone? Alexa opened the front door. Suddenly the lights came on!

"Surprise!" everyone yelled. There was her mom, her dad, her brother, and all her friends. Everyone had remembered!

confused
not sure

Who is telling this story?

    A Alexa

    B Ellen

    C Mom

    D a narrator

> The correct answer is choice D. Alexa is the main character. But she does not tell the story. Ellen and Mom do not tell the story. The story is told by a narrator. The narrator is not a character.

Which character do you know the most about in this story?

A Ellen

B Alexa

C Mom

D Alexa's brother

Alexa is the main character. You know what Alexa is thinking. You know what she does. The other characters are in the story. But you do not know what they think. Choice B is correct.

Suppose Ellen was telling the story. Tell what would be different.

_____

_____

Think about what Ellen knows. Think about what Alexa knows. Here is a sample answer:

> Ellen knows about the surprise party. Alexa does not. And the reader does not. Ellen would tell the reader about the party. The reader could guess how the story ends.

UNIT 3
Craft and Structure

Read this poem. Then answer the questions.

Block City
by Robert Louis Stevenson

1. What are you able
2. To build with your blocks?
3. Castles[1] and palaces,
4. Houses and docks.

5. Rain may keep raining
6. And others may roam[2]
7. But I can be happy
8. While building at home.

Who is probably speaking in this poem?

A a child

B a king

C a builder

D a toy maker

   The correct answer is choice A. The speaker talks about building blocks. He is playing with the blocks. He creates castles, palaces, and other things. He does not need to leave his house. He is happy building with his blocks. The speaker is probably a child.

---

[1]**castles** large homes for kings and queens, like palaces
[2]**roam** to travel around

Which choice *best* describes what the speaker thinks?

A I wish the rain would stop.

B I want to live in a castle.

C I like to make things with my blocks.

D I want some new toys to play with.

Read the poem again. What is the speaker saying? He builds castles and palaces with his blocks. He builds other pretend things, too. He likes to make things with his blocks. Choice C is correct.

How does the speaker feel about the rain? Tell how you know.

_____

_____

Read what the speaker says about rain. Think about the rest of the poem. Here is a sample answer:

The speaker does not care about the rain. He wants to stay inside. The rain does not bother him. He is playing with his blocks.

Test Yourself

Read the story and the poem. Then answer the questions.

What Happened to Reggie?
by Michael Borrow

Reggie was teaching me how to follow tracks. He showed me deer tracks. Then he showed me rabbit tracks.

Finally Reggie said, "Ok, Alex, close your eyes. Count to 100. See if you can follow my tracks."

I did as Reggie said. Then I opened my eyes. Reggie was gone. But I could see his tracks in the snow. I followed them. They led to the barn.

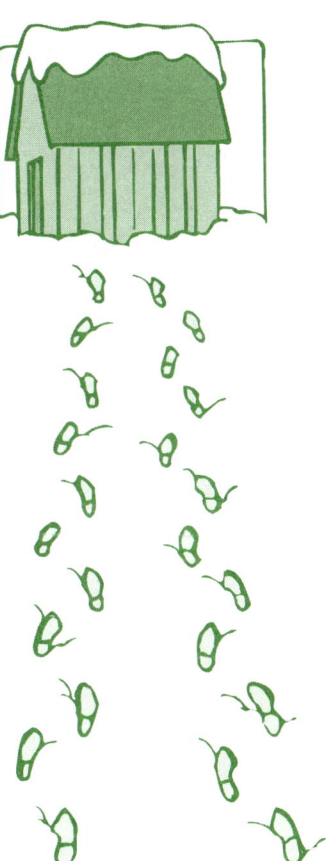

The barn was empty. I noticed another set of tracks. But they were pointing to the barn, too. They were not pointing away from it. It looked like two people had walked to the barn. And no one had walked away. Where was Reggie?

I walked home. Reggie was waiting for me! He laughed. And then he told me how he had tricked me.

"I walked to the barn," he said. "And now watch carefully." Then Reggie started to walk backwards.

A Limerick
by Edward Lear

A limerick is a short, funny poem.

1. There was an Old Man with a beard
2. Who said, "It is just as I feared,
3. Two Owls and a Hen,
4. Four Larks and a Wren[1],
5. Have all built their nests in my beard."

1 Who is telling the story, "What Happened to Reggie?"

   A Reggie

   B Alex

   C Alex's brother

   D someone outside the story

2 From whose point of view is the poem written?

   A the Old Man

   B the owl

   C an outside speaker

   D four larks

---

[1] **owls, hens, larks, wrens** different types of birds

3 How does Alex feel in "What Happened to Reggie?"

   A confused

   B scared

   C sad

   D excited

4 What is the Old Man in the limerick *probably* thinking?

   A It is nice to have birds in my beard.

   B I wish I did not have a beard.

   C I wish these birds would go away.

   D I like owls more than larks.

5 Look at the story, "What Happened to Reggie?" Suppose Reggie was telling the story. What would be different?

_____

_____

_____

_____

Lesson 10

Text Features

RI.1.5, RI.1.6

Vocabulary
exercise
famous
languages
schedule

Nonfiction writing has special **text features.** These are tools for the reader. They help the reader learn more. They make the text easier to use.

Table of Contents and Glossary

The **table of contents** is at the beginning of a book. It shows the chapters in the book. It tells what page they start on. The **glossary** is at the end of the book. It lists words in ABC order. It tells their meanings, like a dictionary. It lists the **key words.** These are words that are important. They might be new to you.

All Kinds of Frogs
Table of Contents

1 What are Frogs? 5
2 The Life of a Frog 12
3 Frogs Around the World 25
4 Dangerous Frogs 33
5 Frogs as Pets 39
Glossary 45

Glossary

gills	body parts that help some animals breath under water
poison	a liquid that some animals use to protect themselves
tadpole	a young frog
toe pads	parts of a frog's toes that help it hold onto surfaces
webbed toes	toes that have pieces of skin connecting them

UNIT 3 Craft and Structure

Text Features

Some writers use **headings.** Headings break up text. They tell you what smaller sections are about. Headings are usually in **bold** print. Read the headings before you read the text. They help you know what you will be reading about.

Pictures give more information. Drawings show information, too. They help you see what the writer is talking about. Sometimes a picture has a **caption.** It tells what the picture is about. Always look at the pictures and drawings. Sometimes they have more information. They may tell you things that are not in the text.

Look at this text. It is from the book *All Kinds of Frogs*.

Hiding from Enemies

Frogs have enemies. Enemies are other animals that try to hurt frogs.

Some frogs use their skin to hide. There are frogs that can change colors. They can blend into a tree. Frogs have bumpy skin. This makes them hard to see when they are on the ground.

This frog is hard to see in the water. He uses the plants in the water. They cover him up.

Look at the heading, "Hiding from Enemies." It is bold. It tells you what this section is about.

Look at the picture. It helps you think of how a frog hides. The caption tells you something new.

Menus and Icons

Web pages have text features, too. **Menus** and **icons** help readers find more information. Readers click on an icon. Then they can read more information. Readers click on a menu. Then they get a list. The list drops down. It gives the reader more choices.

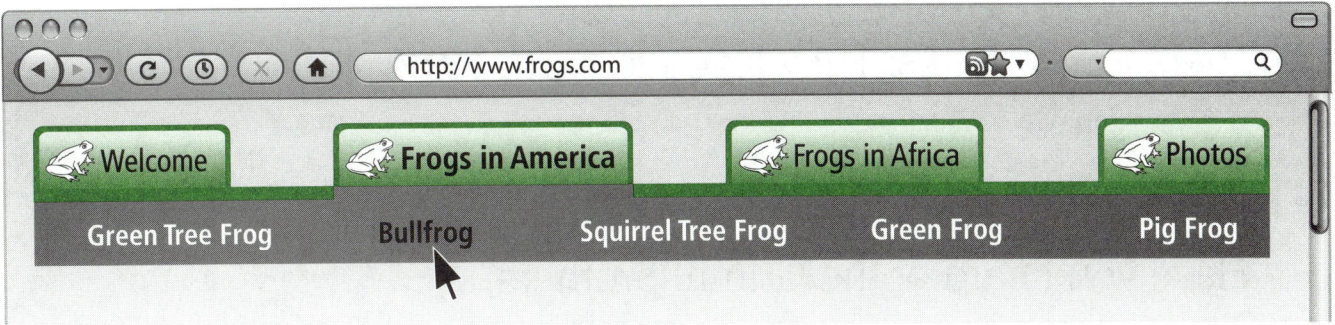

Click on the icon for "Frogs in America." A menu opens. It shows names of frogs in America. You can find out more about bullfrogs. Click on "Bullfrog." Then more information will show on the screen.

Guided Practice

Read the two passages. Then answer the questions.

Passage 1

The Brothers Grimm

Jakob and Wilhelm Grimm were brothers. They lived in Germany a long time ago. The brothers loved books. They loved to read. And they loved to learn.

The Fairy Tales

Have you heard of the Grimm brothers? You have definitely heard some of their stories. "Cinderella." "Snow White and the Seven Dwarfs." "The Frog Prince." "Sleeping Beauty." The Grimm brothers wrote all these stories down. But they did not make the stories up. The stories were around for a long time.

"Snow White and the Seven Dwarfs" is one of the most famous stories.

famous
well-known

Many years ago, people made up fairy tales. They told them to their children. The children grew up. And then they told the stories to their children. The stories were never written down. People remembered them.

The Grimm brothers knew these stories. They had heard them when they were little. They decided to write the stories on paper. They wanted to get the stories right. So they traveled around Germany. They listened to people tell the stories. Then they wrote them down.

The brothers made books of the fairy tales. Many people bought the books. There were over 200 stories in the books.

The Stories Today

People still read the Grimm brothers' stories. Some of them have been made into movies. They have been retold in 160 languages. People all over the world love these stories.

Jakob and Wilhelm were very close. They did many things together.

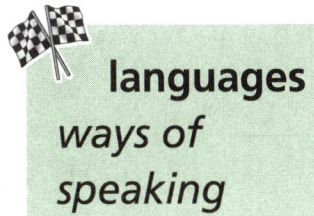

languages
ways of speaking

Passage 2

Fairy Tales for All!

Tell Us About Your Favorite Grimm Story
We want to know which fairy tale you like best! Why is it your favorite?
Click here: [Submit]

People in Germany had many fairy tales. But no one had ever written them down. The Grimm brothers loved the stories. They decided to write them down.

The brothers' names were Jakob and Wilhelm. They traveled around Germany. They listened to people tell stories. Then they wrote them down. They were very careful. They wanted the stories to be right.

The fairy tales were very popular. Many people read them. They are still popular today. There have been movies made of the stories. Movies make the stories fun to watch.

Click the icons at the top. You can learn more about the brothers Grimm. And you can learn about their stories.

Glossary
fairy tale — a made-up story with magic in it
popular — well-liked

Passage 1 is *probably* a _____.

   A web page

   B magazine article

   C glossary

   D book

> Passage 1 is not a web page. There are no icons or menus. It is not a glossary. It does not show words and their meanings. It is not a book. It is too short. It is probably an article in a magazine. Choice B is correct.

What is passage 2?

   A a textbook

   B a table of contents

   C a poem

   D a web page

> The correct answer is choice D. A textbook would have headings. A table of contents shows page numbers. And it shows chapter names. A poem has short lines of text. It usually rhymes. This is a web page. It has icons. And it has menus.

Look at passage 2. You want to read one of the fairy tales. Which icon should you click?

A Welcome

B The Brothers

C The Fairy Tales

D Movies

> Think about what each icon probably shows. You can see what "Welcome" shows. "The Brothers" probably tells more about the Grimm brothers. "Movies" probably talks about movies made from the stories. Click "The Fairy Tales." You will probably be able to read some of the stories. Choice C is the correct answer.

Look at passage 2. What text feature helps you find the meaning of popular?

_____

_____

> Think about what the text features do. Here is a sample answer:

The glossary tells the meanings of words. It shows what popular means.

Look at passage 1. Look at the picture of the brothers. Read the caption. What can you learn from the picture? What can you learn from the caption? Can you learn this in the passage, too?

_____

_____

_____

_____

_____

 The picture helps you see something. The caption tells you more about the brothers. Here is a sample answer:

> The picture shows what the brothers looked like. The caption tells that they were close. The passage does not tell you what they looked like. You have to look at the picture to find out.

Test Yourself

Read two passages. Then answer the questions.

Passage 1

Field Day Fun!

A field day is a fun day at school. You play games. You have races. You work as a team with your class. Plus you get to spend time outside. And you get exercise.

exercise *moving your body*

How can I plan a field day?

First, talk to your teacher. Make sure it is ok. Field days are fun when the entire school plays. But you can have a field day with just your class, too. Your teacher can help you make plans. Field days are a lot of work. Make sure you have a good plan and enough helpers. Make sure you have the supplies you need. Then everyone will have fun.

How long is field day?

Field day can be a whole school day. Or it can be part of a day. Talk to your teacher. Find out what is best.

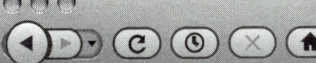

What do we do on field day?

Whatever you want! Well, kind of. Make a schedule. This tells you what games you will play. It tells what times you will play the games. Pick some games. Look on this web page to find ideas. You can play games. You can have races. You can even have fun contests. Do whatever works best for your class.

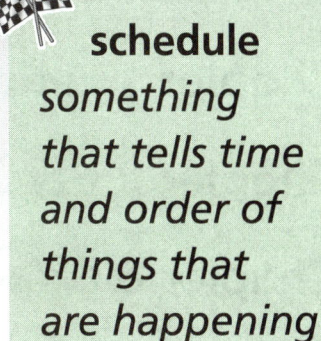

schedule *something that tells time and order of things that are happening*

Who wins field day?

Everyone! You can have winners for races. And you can have winners for games. You can give out ribbons. But field day is mostly about having fun. It is not about winning or losing. Make sure everyone has a good time.

The sack race is a fun game for field day.

Click on the icons above. They will give you ideas. Be creative!

 Click here. Read about other people's field days. Tell us about your field day.

Passage 2

Have a Healthy Life!
Table of Contents

Chapter 1 Eating Healthy 2

Chapter 2 Getting Exercise 15

Chapter 3 Exercising Your Mind 26

Chapter 4 Making Good Friends 40

Chapter 5 Trying New Things 48

Glossary 52

Glossary

Community	a group of people that live and work together
Exercise	moving your body
Friendship	being friends with someone
Journal	a book to write about things
Talent	something you are good at

1 Look at passage 1. Which text feature helps you tell about your field day?

   A picture

   B headings

   C icon

   D menu

2 Which of these text features is *not* in passage 1?

   A table of contents

   B headings

   C menu

   D picture

3 Look at passage 2. You are reading the book *Have a Healthy Life!* Which text feature would you use to find what a word means?

_____

_____

4 What information can you find in the table of contents?

    A word meanings

    B chapter names

    C pictures

    D field day stories

5 Look at passage 1. Tell what you find out from the picture. Can you find this out from the text, too?

_____

_____

_____

_____

6 Which of these *best* describes how the information in passage 1 is organized?

　A textbook page

　B diary entry

　C magazine article

　D web page

7 Look at passage 1. How do the headings help you find information?

_____

_____

_____

_____

REVIEW

Craft and Structure

Unit 3

Vocabulary
community
explore
sternly

Read the passage. Then answer the questions.

Living on the Sea

Can you imagine a floating city? That is what *Freedom Ship* will be! A group of people came up with an idea. It is a community that lives on the sea. It travels around the world.

community a group of people living together

Onboard the Ship

What will be on the ship? Everything you can think of! People will live on the ship. There will be homes and parks. There will be places to shop. There will also be places to work. There will be libraries and banks. And there will be schools.

The ship will be huge. People will be able to ride a train on the ship. It will take them from one place to another. Everything you need to live will be on *Freedom Ship*.

Leaving the Ship

People on *Freedom Ship* do not have to stay on the ship. They can get off. They can explore new places. The ship will stop in many countries. People can visit these countries. There will be an airport on the ship. People can fly off the ship. There will also be a place to park boats.

explore
to look at and discover

Around the World

Freedom Ship will sail around the world. It will make stops. But it will not stay. It will keep moving. It will go all the way around the world every two years.

Freedom Ship has not been built yet. But the people are working hard. Maybe you will live there when you grow up.

1 You would *probably* find this passage in ____.

   A a history book

   B a news magazine

   C a book of poetry

   D a book of fairy tales

2 Look at the picture. What can you learn from the picture?

   A what will be on *Freedom Ship*

   B what *Freedom Ship* will look like

   C where *Freedom Ship* will go

   D where people will live on *Freedom Ship*

3 The text feature "Around the World" is ____.

   A a heading

   B an icon

   C a menu

   D a glossary

Read the story. Then answer the questions.

What a Day!
by Bethany Fiore

Tuesday was quite a day. First, I forgot to set my alarm clock. I woke up late. I tried to hurry. But I missed my bus.

"I have a meeting this morning," Mom said. "You will have to walk to school."

I tried to walk fast. But I was late to school.

I was looking forward to lunch. All morning, the sun was shining. I could not wait to go outside. We always go outside after we eat. I was eating the last bite of lunch. Just then, it started to rain.

"Sorry, class, you will have to stay inside today," said my teacher.

The afternoon went slowly. Then my best friend passed me a note. My teacher did not see who passed it. But she saw me pick it up.

"Jenny, come to the front of the class," she said sternly. "Read the note to the class."

My face turned bright red. I could not wait to go home.

Finally, I got off the bus. I just wanted to go to my room. I was thinking about my bad day. The best part of the day was my new shoes. I was thinking so hard that I didn't see the big puddle.

SPLASH!

sternly
in a firm way

4 Who is telling this story?

　A Mom

　B the teacher

　C Jenny

　D Jenny's best friend

5 Where would you *probably* find this story?

　A in a children's magazine

　B in a science book

　C in a note from a friend

　D in a newspaper

6 What happens at the beginning of the story?

　A Jenny eats lunch.

　B Jenny sleeps late.

　C Jenny has to read a note aloud.

　D Jenny goes home.

7 What is the setting of the story? How does the picture help you?

_____

_____

_____

Like You Have Never Seen Before!

Australia is a country. It is also a huge island. Australia is full of lots of special animals. Most of them are only found in Australia!

This kangaroo has its baby in its pouch. A kangaroo baby is called a joey.

Have you ever seen a kangaroo? Kangaroos live in Australia. They are a kind of marsupial. A marsupial is an animal with a pouch. The babies live in the pouch. They stay there until they are bigger.

Australia has a lot of birds. There are some that cannot fly! A cassowary is a bird in Australia. It is very big. It cannot fly. But it can jump high. And it can swim very well.

Do you want to know more? Read about other animals in Australia. Click on the icons above.

A cassowary is the biggest bird that cannot fly.

8 Which text feature helps you find what a joey is?

    A icon

    B menu

    C picture

    D caption

9 Which icon would you *probably* use to read more about the kangaroo?

    A Reptiles

    B Land Animals

    C Sea Animals

    D Birds

10 Look at the picture of the cassowary. What can you find out only from the picture? What can you find out only from the text?

_____

_____

_____

_____

UNIT 3
Craft and Structure

Integration of Knowledge and Ideas

Sometimes you read things with pictures. The pictures help you see new things. They help you understand what you read. You might learn something that was not in the text.

You can compare things when you read two stories. Think about what is the same. Think about what is different. This helps you understand the stories.

This unit is about how you find information in what you read. It is about using that information. And it is about learning new things.

- **In Lesson 11,** you will learn how pictures help you understand what you read. You will look at the pictures to learn new things.

- **Lesson 12** is about facts and opinions. You will learn how to tell if something has proof.

- **In Lesson 13,** you will look at two texts. You will find what is the same about them. And you will find what is different about them.

Visual Literacy

Lesson 11

RL.1.7, RI.1.7

Vocabulary
chores
dwarf
moisture
protect
requirement
stalls

Look at a book that you like. Are there pictures in it? The pictures help you understand the book better. Charts and maps can also help you learn. These things add meaning to the words that you read.

Guided Practice

Read the story. Then answer the questions.

A New Friend

Beth opened her eyes. Then she squeezed them shut again. She did not want to get out of bed. It was still dark outside. Beth sighed. Then she rolled out of bed.

There were many chores to do on the farm. She had to do her share. Then she had to get ready for school. Beth did not like her new home. Her family had moved from New York City. She missed the city. She missed her friends. And she missed sleeping in.

"Your father has something to show you," Beth's mom said.

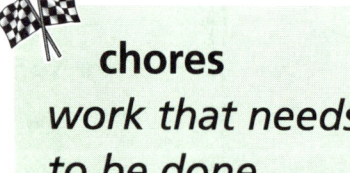

chores
work that needs to be done

Beth walked toward the barn. She wondered what her father wanted to show her. He probably wanted her to do a new chore.

Beth opened the barn door. Her dad looked up at her.

"Beth," he said, "Come with me. I want to show you something."

They walked beside the stalls. Beth yawned. Suddenly, she heard a noise. The noise was not from the cows. It was not from the chickens. Then a beautiful horse stuck her head out of a stall. She looked right at Beth.

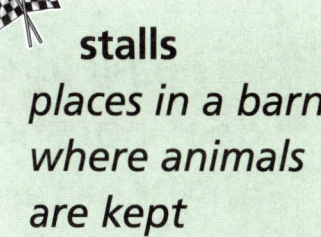

stalls
places in a barn where animals are kept

"Oh!" Beth cried. "She's amazing!"

"I need a horse for the farm," her dad said. "But if you help to take care of her, you can ride her. And you can give her a name."

Beth reached her hand out. The horse put her nose in Beth's hand. Maybe the farm was not so bad after all.

Look at the picture. What detail is *best* shown by this picture?

    A Beth is afraid of the horse.

    B Beth likes the horse.

    C Beth has to do chores on the farm.

    D Beth goes to school after her chores.

> The picture does not show Beth doing chores. It does not show Beth going to school. Beth is not afraid of the horse. She is holding out her hand. She likes the horse. Choice B is correct.

What do you think one of Beth's chores might be?

_____

_____

_____

> Look at the picture. Beth is carrying a basket. Think about something she might need a basket for. Here is a sample answer:

    Beth has a basket. She lives on a farm. The picture shows chickens. She might need to gather eggs.

UNIT 4
Integration of Knowledge and Ideas

What can you learn from the picture that is *not* in the story?

_____

_____

_____

_____

 Look at what Beth is wearing. Here is a sample answer:

> Beth is wearing a dress and a bonnet. The story takes place long ago. The story does not say when it takes place. I can tell this by the picture.

Read the passage. Then answer the questions.

A Dwarf Planet

Earth is a planet. It travels around the sun. Mars is a planet, too. There are eight planets in all. People used to think there were nine planets. They thought Pluto was a planet. But Pluto is not a planet. It is a dwarf planet.

dwarf
small

People do not know much about Pluto. It is very far away. Scientists are learning more. In 2006, they decided Pluto was not a planet. Scientists said there are three requirements for a planet. Dwarf planets only have two of the requirements.

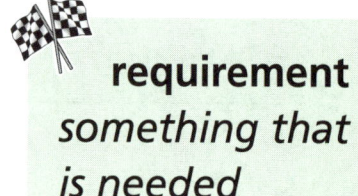
requirement
something that is needed

Pluto is farther from the sun than the planets. It is smaller, too. In fact, Pluto is smaller than the moon. There are other things in space that are the same size as Pluto. They are not planets either.

Many people do not like that Pluto is called a dwarf planet. They think it should still be called a planet. Scientists are learning more about Pluto. Maybe someday it will be called a planet again.

Which of these is *best* shown by the picture?

   A the sizes of the planets and Pluto
   B what a dwarf planet is
   C when Pluto was discovered
   D the size of the moon

> The picture shows the planets. And it shows Pluto. It shows the sizes of each one. You can see which are big planets. And you can see which are small. Choice A is correct.

Name one detail from the text that is *not* shown in the picture.

_____

_____

> There are a few ways to answer this. Look at the picture. And read the text carefully. Here is a sample answer:

   The text says that Pluto is smaller than Earth's moon. The picture does not show the moon. So I cannot see the sizes of Pluto and the moon.

Imagine you wrote this passage. You want to put another picture with the passage. What might you make the picture of? How would this help someone understand the passage?

___

 You could make different pictures. Think of an important detail. Decide how a picture would help you understand it better. Here is a sample answer:

> One detail is that there are other things in space that are the same size as Pluto. I would make a picture to show these other things. Then you could see what they are. And you could look at their sizes and Pluto's size.

Test Yourself

Read the story. Then answer the questions.

The Roller Coaster

I looked up. Way up. The roller coaster was huge! I had told all my friends that I was going to ride it. I had bragged about how excited I was. Now the time had come. And I did not feel very good.

"We do not need to ride it, Marcus," Dad said. "It is the fastest roller coaster in the park. It is the highest, too. We can try another roller coaster first."

"No," I said firmly. "I want to ride the Dominator. It is going to be my first roller coaster."

My stomach did a flip. I looked at my shoes. I looked at the roller coaster. I looked at the sky. I looked at Dad. He was looking at me.

"Do you want to get in line?" he asked.

"Yes," I said out loud.

"No," my brain said.

Dad and I walked toward the end of the line. I took a deep breath. My stomach was tied in knots.

"Excuse me," said a man at the end of the line. He held a measuring stick. He put it next to me.

"I'm sorry. You're not tall enough to ride," he said.

"Oh," I said. "Let's go ride the Giant Swing, Dad."

Suddenly my stomach felt a lot better.

1 Look at the first picture. What detail does this picture show?

   A Marcus was excited.

   B Marcus was scared.

   C Dad wanted to ride the roller coaster.

   D Dad thought the roller coaster was boring.

2 Look at the second picture. How does Marcus feel at the end of the story? How does the picture help you know this?

_____

_____

_____

_____

3 Use the pictures and the story. Describe the setting of the story.

_____

_____

_____

_____

Smile Big!

Look in a mirror and smile. What do you see? Rows of teeth. Your teeth are very important. They help you eat. So it is important to take care of your teeth.

The outside of a tooth is enamel. It is very hard. It has to be hard so you can bite your food. Pulp is inside the tooth. The pulp gives moisture. It also helps protect tissues in the teeth. The gums keep the tooth in place. Gums are pink and soft.

You are not born with teeth. Your teeth start to come in when you are very young. First you get baby teeth. Then your baby teeth start to come out. You get adult teeth in their place.

You use your teeth every day. So they get dirty. You must clean them so they stay healthy. Use a toothbrush to clean your teeth. It helps clean all around your teeth. Use floss to clean the space between your teeth. And make sure you go to the dentist. She will help you learn to keep your teeth clean.

moisture
wetness

protect
to keep safe

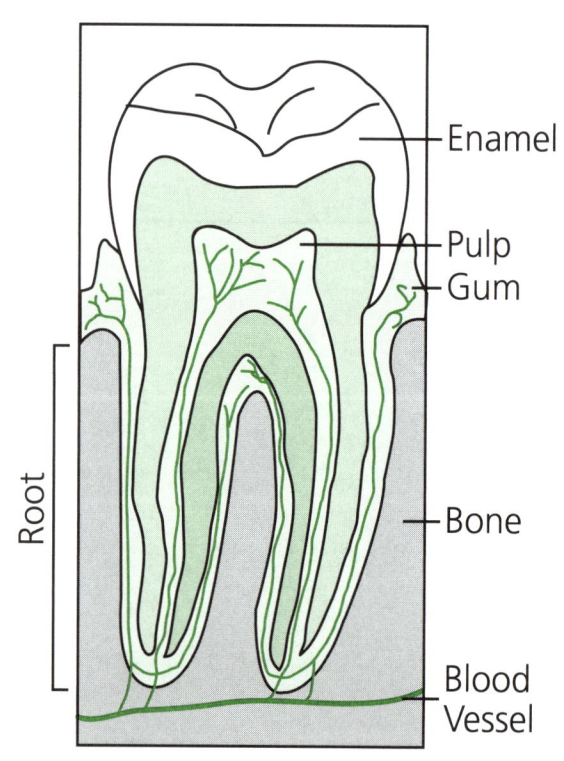

4 What does the picture show you?

_____

_____

_____

_____

5 Look at the picture. Tell about something you can only learn about in the picture.

_____

_____

_____

_____

6 Which of these details is *not* in the picture?

   A Enamel is on the outside of the tooth.

   B Pulp is inside the tooth.

   C Baby teeth come before adult teeth.

   D The gum is around the tooth.

UNIT 4
Integration of Knowledge and Ideas

Identifying Connections

Lesson 12

RI.1.8

Vocabulary
burrow
published

Authors write to tell you something. They must back up what they write. They do this with facts. A **fact** is a true statement. It can be proven.

An author might write about what he thinks or believes. This is his **opinion.** An opinion is not a fact. It cannot be proven. These key words help you find an opinion.

| I think | best | worst | everyone |
| never | always | no one | |

Look for facts and opinions. This helps you understand what you read. You will know if the author backs up what she writes.

An author can give his opinion. But he needs to use facts, too. Facts help show he understands what he is writing.

Look for connections when you read. Ask yourself *why* things happen. Ask yourself *how* they happen, too.

Look for cause and effect. The cause is why something happens. The effect is what happens.

> Anita forgot her watch. So she was late for dinner.

The effect is that Anita was late for dinner. Why was she late for dinner? She forgot her watch. That is the cause.

Guided Practice

Read the passage. Then answer the questions.

The Groundhog's Shadow

It is cold outside. There is snow on the ground. When will it be spring? Ask a groundhog!

February 2 is Groundhog Day. It started because of a story told for many years. It says a groundhog can tell what the weather will be. He comes out of his burrow on February 2. Sometimes he sees his shadow. Then there will be six more weeks of winter. Sometimes he does not see his shadow. Then spring will be early.

One town is famous for Groundhog Day. Punxsutawney (pungk•suh•TAW•nee), Pennsylvania, has a famous groundhog. His name is Phil. He comes out on Groundhog Day.

burrow
a hole where an animal lives

Many people come to see Phil. They want to know what he will say. They also come to have fun. There is a big party for Groundhog Day.

There is a club that takes care of Phil. The people dress up on Groundhog Day. They wear top hats.

Many other towns have special groundhogs. But the people in Punxsutawney only listen to Phil. They are proud of Phil. Phil is never wrong. He is the only groundhog that can tell the weather.

So, how will you know when spring is coming? Wait for February 2. See what Phil has to say!

Which sentence from the passage is an opinion?

    A One town is famous for Groundhog Day.

    B His name is Phil.

    C Phil is never wrong.

    D They wear top hats.

> An opinion cannot be proved. A fact is a true statement. Choices A, B, and D are facts. Choice C is an opinion. The club thinks Phil is never wrong. Other people might think he is wrong sometimes. Choice C is correct.

Phil sees his shadow. This is a cause. What is the effect?

    A There will be six more weeks of winter.

    B There will be an early spring.

    C There will be a big party.

    D People will wear top hats.

> The correct answer is A. Look at the second paragraph. It tells you what happens. Phil sees his shadow. Then there will be six more weeks of winter. The word *then* helps you find the effect.

Tell why Groundhog Day started.

_____

_____

_____

_____

 You need to use cause and effect. You are also connecting ideas. Here is a sample answer:

> Groundhog Day started because of a story. People told the story for a long time. Then they made a day to celebrate it. The story says that groundhogs can tell the weather.

Read this sentence from the passage.

He is the only groundhog that can tell the weather.

Is this a fact or an opinion? Tell how you know.

_____

_____

_____

_____

 Read the other sentences around this one. Can you prove this? Here is a sample answer:

> This is an opinion. People in other towns think their groundhogs are right. The people in Punxsutawney think Phil is right. Some people probably think none of them are right. You cannot prove this. So it is an opinion.

UNIT 4
Integration of Knowledge and Ideas

Test Yourself

Read the passage. Then answer the questions.

Peggy Parish
by Jonah Mann

My favorite author is Peggy Parish. She wrote the Amelia Bedelia books. They are the funniest books. Plus they help you learn, too.

Peggy Parish was born in 1927. She loved to read. She decided to become a teacher. But she really wanted to write books.

Finally, Peggy had her first book published. Then she wrote the first Amelia Bedelia book. Everyone loved it! So she began to write more. She wrote 12 books about Amelia Bedelia in all.

published
to be printed and sold

Amelia Bedelia is a maid. She works for Mr. and Mrs. Rogers. She does exactly what they tell her to do. And I mean, exactly. Mrs. Rogers asked Amelia to "dust the furniture." So Amelia put dust all over the furniture. Mrs. Rogers told her to "draw the drapes." So Amelia drew a picture of the curtains. Sometimes Amelia gets into trouble. But things work out in the end.

Peggy died in 1988. But everyone wanted more Amelia Bedelia books. So her nephew began to write more books. He gave Amelia Bedelia new adventures.

1. Which of these is a fact?

    A My favorite author is Peggy Parish.

    B Peggy Parish was born in 1927.

    C They are the funniest books.

    D But everyone wanted more Amelia Bedelia books.

2. Why does Amelia sometimes get in trouble?

    A She does exactly what she is told.

    B She is a maid.

    C She loves to read.

    D She does not like Mrs. Rogers.

3. What are three facts about Peggy Parish?

    Fact 1: _____

    _____

    Fact 2: _____

    _____

    Fact 3: _____

    _____

4 Which of these is an opinion?

   A Peggy had her first book published.

   B She decided to become a teacher.

   C She wrote 12 books about Amelia Bedelia in all.

   D Everyone loved it!

5 The author says, "They are the funniest books." Tell why he thinks they are funny.

_____

_____

_____

_____

6 Read this sentence.

   So her nephew began to write more books.

   This is an effect. What was the cause?

_____

_____

UNIT 4
Integration of Knowledge and Ideas

Lesson 13: Comparing and Contrasting

RL.1.9, RI.1.9

Vocabulary
- coach
- comet
- enemy
- politics
- rescue
- scent
- trapper
- wrestled

You read different types of writing. **Nonfiction** is information. You read it to find out about something. **Fiction** is made-up. It is the stories you read. **Realistic fiction** is a story that could happen in real life. **Traditional stories** have been around for a long time. These are traditional stories:

folktales	stories that teach a lesson about how people act
fairy tales	stories with magic
fables	stories with animals that act like people
myths	stories that explain something

Sometimes two stories are alike. But they have differences, too. Many stories have things in common. Think of the story "Beauty and the Beast." Then think of the story "Sleeping Beauty." They are not about the same thing. But there are some things that are alike. Both stories have magic. A character is changed. Only true love can break a spell. There are also differences.

UNIT 4
Integration of Knowledge and Ideas

The Beast was changed from a beast to a prince. Sleeping Beauty fell asleep for a long time.

Stories can seem very different. But you might find parts that are alike.

Guided Practice

Read two stories. Then answer the questions.

Passage 1

Toads and Diamonds
a French fairy tale

Once there was a woman. She had two daughters. The older daughter was mean and rude. The younger daughter was kind and sweet. But the mother loved her older daughter best. She made the younger daughter work hard.

One day, the younger daughter went to the stream. She filled her jug with water. Then a poor, old woman appeared.

"May I have a drink?" the woman asked.

"Yes!" the younger daughter said. She quickly gave the woman a drink.

The woman was actually a fairy. She wanted to thank the girl. So she gave her a gift. Jewels and flowers would fall out of the girl's mouth every time she spoke.

The younger daughter went home. She told her mother what happened. And roses and diamonds fell out of her mouth.

The mother wanted her favorite daughter to get a gift. She told the older daughter to go to the woods. She told her to give a drink to the poor woman. The older daughter complained. She did not want to do work. But she went.

The older daughter went to the same stream. A beautiful princess appeared.

"May I have a drink?" the princess asked.

"I do not work for you," the older daughter said. "Get your own drink."

The princess was the same fairy. She did not like the older daughter. So she gave the daughter a different gift.

The older daughter went home. She told her mother what happened. Toads and snakes fell out of her mouth.

The mother was very upset. She blamed her younger daughter. She kicked her out of the house. The younger daughter did not know where to go. She began to cry.

Soon a prince came along. He asked the girl why she was crying. She told him. And pearls and lilies fell out of her mouth. The prince fell in love with the girl. He took her home. And they were married.

Passage 2

Cinderella

an adaptation

Once there was a girl named Cinderella. She lived with her stepmother and her two stepsisters. They were very mean to her. They made her work hard. She was never able to do anything fun. But Cinderella was a kind and sweet girl.

The prince decided to have a ball. He invited all the people in the land. Cinderella's stepmother and stepsisters were very excited. Cinderella wanted to go to the ball, too. But her stepmother would not let her.

The stepmother and stepsisters left for the ball. Cinderella sat down. She cried and cried. Suddenly Cinderella's fairy godmother appeared.

"Why are you crying?" she asked Cinderella.

Cinderella told her about the ball. The fairy godmother pulled out her wand. In a moment, she turned a pumpkin into a coach. And Cinderella was wearing a beautiful dress. She looked at her feet. She had on beautiful glass slippers.

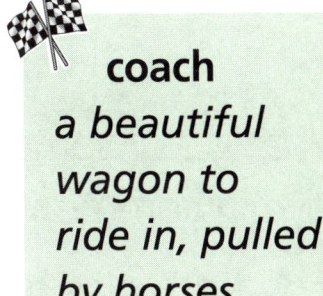

coach
a beautiful wagon to ride in, pulled by horses

"Have fun at the ball," said the fairy godmother. "But you must leave by midnight. Or your coach will turn back into a pumpkin. And your dress will turn back to rags."

Cinderella went to the ball. Everyone noticed her. The prince danced with her. They fell in love. Suddenly the clock chimed midnight. Cinderella remembered what her fairy godmother had said. She ran from the palace. She ran so fast that she lost one of her glass slippers.

The prince wanted to find her. But he did not know her name. He found the glass slipper. He said he would marry the girl who fit the glass slipper.

All the girls wanted to try on the shoe. Cinderella's stepsisters tried it on. But it did not fit. Finally it was Cinderella's turn. The shoe fit perfectly!

Everyone was surprised! The prince and Cinderella were married. And they lived happily ever after.

What is *not* something the two passages have in common?

A Both girls have mean mothers.

B Both girls must work hard.

C Both girls get water from a stream.

D Both girls meet a fairy.

In passage 1, the younger daughter gets water. In passage 2, Cinderella does not get water. The other choices are the same in both passages. Choice C is correct.

How are the ends of the stories the same?

_____

_____

_____

_____

 Look back at the stories. Find what is the same. Here is a sample answer:

> Both girls marry a prince. The princes save the girls from bad things. In the first story, the prince helps the girl. She does not have any place to live. In the second story, the prince gets Cinderella away from her stepmother.

What are three things that are different between these stories?

1. _____

   _____

2. _____

   _____

3. _____

   _____

> ✓ Think about what is different. Here is a sample answer:

1. In story 1, the girl has one sister. In story 2, Cinderella has two stepsisters.

2. In story 1, the fairy's gift lasts forever. In story 2, the fairy's gift lasts until midnight.

3. In story 1, the people do not go to a ball. In story 2, they go to a ball.

UNIT 4
Integration of Knowledge and Ideas

Nonfiction

Two informational texts can be alike, too. The authors might use the same facts. But they tell them in different ways. They might write the story of a person's life. This is called a **biography.** They might write about just one event. You can compare how texts are the same. And you can see how they are different.

Guided Practice

Read two passages. Then answer the questions.

Passage 1

Davy Crockett: A Biography

Davy Crockett was born on August 17, 1786. He was born in Tennessee. His family lived in a log cabin. Davy liked to go hunting. He did not like to go to school. He ran away from home when he was young. He learned to be a good hunter and trapper. He liked to be in the woods.

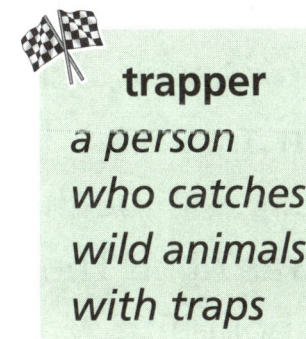

trapper
a person who catches wild animals with traps

Davy joined the army in 1813. Davy was a scout. This meant he went out by himself. He looked at what the enemy was doing. Then he told the leaders.

enemy
the people you are against

Next, Davy decided to work in politics. He was elected to the House of Representatives. Davy did not always agree with people. Sometimes he argued with them. But he always said what he thought was right.

politics *work in the government*

Davy decided to go to Texas. Texas was not part of the United States yet. It was part of Mexico. But it wanted to be its own country. A group of men went to Texas. They wanted to help Texas fight to be free. Davy went with them. They went to a fort called the Alamo.

The Mexican army attacked the Alamo. It was a hard fight. The Texans lost the fight. Almost everyone in the Alamo died. Davy Crockett died there on March 6, 1836.

Davy Crockett is remembered for many things. He wore a coonskin cap. He fought for what he thought was right. There are many stories about him. Many of them are not true. They say he did things that people cannot really do. But he also did do many great things.

Passage 2

Davy Crockett's Stories

Davy Crockett loved the woods. He was a hunter and a trapper. He was a soldier. He worked in the government. And he loved to tell stories about things he did. The stories were not always true. This is a look at Davy's life through his stories.

Davy began hunting when he was just three years old. One day, a bear came into the house. The bear started eating some food. So little Davy wrestled the bear to the ground.

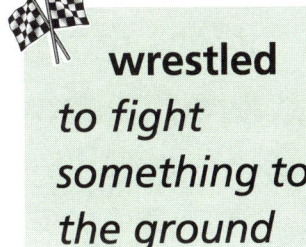

wrestled
to fight something to the ground

Everyone knew Davy was a good hunter. Even the animals knew. They did not wait for Davy to hunt them. They just gave up when they saw him coming.

Davy had a silly grin. Davy grinned at a raccoon in a tree. The raccoon began to laugh and laugh. It fell out of the tree. Then Davy caught it.

One day, Davy was riding on his pet alligator. The enemy was all around him. He rode straight up a waterfall to get away.

It was the middle of May. Everything was covered in snow and ice. Davy knew something was wrong. He went to the North Pole. A comet was stuck on the North Pole. Earth could not turn. Davy grabbed the comet. He swung it around. Then he threw it back into space. Earth started moving again. Everything warmed up.

And that is how Davy saved the world. Or so he said.

comet
an object from space with a long tail

What subject do these two passages have in common?

    A the battle of the Alamo

    B how Davy wrestled a bear

    C Davy's pet alligator

    D Davy's life

> Choice A is only in passage 1. Choices B and C are only in passage 2. Both passages talk about Davy's life. Choice D is correct.

What is one fact from passage 2 that is *not* in passage 1?

    A Davy loved to tell stories.

    B Davy was a soldier.

    C Davy was a hunter.

    D Davy liked to be in the woods.

> Choices B, C, and D are in both passages. Only passage 2 says that Davy liked to tell stories. So choice A is correct.

Integration of Knowledge and Ideas

These passages work together. Tell how they do this.

_____
_____
_____
_____
_____

✓ Both passages tell about Davy's life. Look at the information in both. Here is a sample answer:

> Davy did a lot of things. Passage 1 tells just facts. It says that people told stories about Davy. Passage 2 tells stories that Davy told. They are probably like some of the stories other people told. Both passages help you understand all about Davy Crockett.

How is the picture in passage 1 different from the one in passage 2?

___

___

___

___

 Look at the picture in passage 1. Look at the picture in passage 2. Here is a sample answer:

> The picture in passage 1 is a painting. It was probably made when Davy was alive. It is close to what he really looked like. The picture in passage 2 is a drawing. It was probably done closer to today. The person was just guessing at what he looked like.

UNIT 4
Integration of Knowledge and Ideas

Test Yourself

Read two passages. Then answer the questions.

Passage 1

Dogs to the Rescue

Snow is a lot of fun. But it can also be unsafe. Sometimes people are hurt in the snow. Sometimes no one else knows where they are. Then dogs help to save them. Dogs can find lost people fast.

rescue
to save

Rescue dogs have to be trained. They work hard. They learn how to follow a scent. They learn how to dig to find someone. They learn how to obey.

scent
a smell

Dogs have very good noses. They can smell things that people cannot smell. They sniff around an area. They find the scent of a person. The scent leaves a trail. The dog can follow the trail. And then he can find the person.

UNIT 4
Integration of Knowledge and Ideas

Sometimes people are buried under snow. The dog can still follow the scent. Then the dog can start to dig. She can dig the person out. Then the rescue people can help.

A rescue dog has to pay attention. Dogs like to run and play. But a rescue dog must know when to work. He must listen to people. He knows he will get a treat later. He can play later. But first he has to do his job.

Rescue dogs are important. They help to find lost people. They can work faster than the rescue workers. They save many lives.

Passage 2

Saved by the Dog

January 24—

Yesterday, a dog saved a young boy's life. It looked like a perfect day for skiing. Seven-year-old Ethan Turner was skiing with his family. He got ahead of his father on the trail. Then he took a wrong turn. Soon he was lost.

His parents told the ski patrol. The ski patrol quickly started looking for Ethan. They used their rescue dogs. The dogs followed Ethan's scent. They used the smell to look for him.

It took the patrol about an hour to find Ethan. The dogs work hard to find a person fast. Without the dogs, it would have taken much longer. They may never have found Ethan.

Coby is a three-year-old husky. She found Ethan. He was very cold. But he was not hurt. The patrol took him back to the ski lodge. Ethan says he wants to get Coby a special treat. He wants to thank her for saving him.

1 Which fact is only found in passage 1?

　A Rescue dogs save people in the snow.

　B Rescue dogs can dig people out of the snow.

　C Ethan was skiing with his family.

　D Children should not go skiing.

2 What is the difference between these two passages?

　A Passage 1 is a report. Passage 2 is a news article.

　B Passage 1 is a story. Passage 2 is a report.

　C Passage 1 is a biography. Passage 2 is a story.

　D Passage 1 is fiction. Passage 2 is nonfiction.

3 Which of the following would describe both passages?

   A Both are stories about skiing.

   B Both are about a boy being saved.

   C Both are about snow storms.

   D Both are about rescue dogs.

4 Tell about a fact that is in both passages.

_____

_____

_____

_____

5 What fact is only found in passage 2?

   A Huskies can be rescue dogs.

   B Rescue dogs work hard.

   C Snow can be unsafe.

   D Dogs have good noses.

REVIEW

Integration of Knowledge and Ideas

Unit 4

Vocabulary
rhyme

Read two passages. Then answer the questions.

Passage 1

How Fly Saved the River

an American Indian legend

Long ago, there was a beautiful river. Many animals drank the water. Moose came to drink the water. But Moose was very big. He drank a lot of water. The other animals began to worry. Moose was drinking all the water.

The animals wanted Moose to leave the river. But Moose was much bigger than them. They were scared of Moose.

Finally, Fly said that he would make Moose leave. The animals laughed. How could a tiny fly scare a big moose? Fly flew away. He had a plan.

Moose came to the river. He began to drink. Fly landed on Moose's leg. He bit hard. Moose stomped his foot. Then Fly began to jump all over Moose. He bit him again and again. Moose shook his head. He ran around. He stomped his feet. But Fly would not go away. Finally Moose ran away from the river. He never came back. Then the other animals had water to drink.

Passage 2

The Lion and the Mouse

an Aesop's fable

One day, Lion was taking a nap. Mouse ran across Lion's paw. Lion woke up. He trapped Mouse with his paw. He wanted to eat Mouse.

"Please, Lion," Mouse said. "Please let me go. Maybe someday I will be able to help you."

Lion laughed and laughed. How could a little mouse help him? He was the king of the jungle. But Lion decided to let Mouse go.

Later, Lion got trapped in a net. He could not get out. Mouse heard Lion roaring. He ran over to Lion. He quickly began to chew through the net. Soon Lion was free.

"Thank you, little friend," Lion said.

1 What is true about both stories?

  A They have rivers.

  B They are in the jungle.

  C They have animals that talk.

  D They have animals that get trapped.

2 What is one difference between Fly in passage 1 and Mouse in passage 2?

  A Fly is laughed at.

  B Fly chases an animal away.

  C Mouse is small.

  D Mouse can talk.

3 What can you see from the picture in passage 2?

  A how small Mouse is

  B how Lion got trapped

  C where the river is

  D how Mouse saved Lion

4 What are two ways that Fly and Mouse are the same?

  1. _____

  2. _____

5 Both of these stories teach a lesson. What lesson do they teach?

_____

_____

_____

_____

Read two passages. Then answer the questions.

Passage 1

My Favorite Book: *Green Eggs and Ham*

by Sam Isaacs

The best book in the world is *Green Eggs and Ham*. It is by Dr. Seuss. My mom bought it for me. I could not read it at first. So Mom read it to me. Then I learned to read. It was the first book I read by myself.

The book is about two characters. One of them is named Sam. He keeps trying to get the other character to eat green eggs and ham. The other keeps saying that he will not eat them. He says he does not like them. Many funny things happen. But Sam keeps asking him. Finally he gets tired of saying no. So he tries the green eggs and ham. It turns out that he likes them!

The book is great. It teaches a good lesson. It tells people to try new things. The book is very funny. I like that one character is named Sam. My name is Sam, too. It is cool that the character has my name.

Passage 2

Dr. Seuss

Dr. Seuss liked to write fun stories. First he drew cartoons. Then he decided to write a book. He began to write children's books. They are funny books. They have words that rhyme. They have interesting characters.

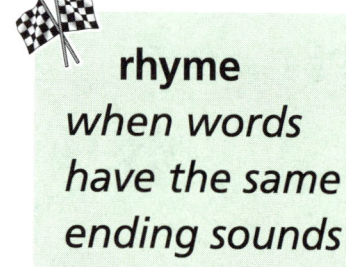

rhyme when words have the same ending sounds

Dr. Seuss also drew pictures for his books. He made up different types of animals. And he made up words. But his books are easy to understand. And they are fun to read.

His books are very popular. Some of them have been made into television shows. Some of them have been made into movies. There are even stuffed animals for some of the characters. One of his most popular books is *Green Eggs and Ham*. Another one is *The Cat in the Hat*. Which is your favorite Dr. Seuss book?

6 Which of these statements in passage 1 is an opinion?

  A I could not read it at first.

  B But Sam keeps asking him.

  C So he tried the green eggs and ham.

  D It is cool that the character has my name.

7 What does the picture in passage 2 show you?

  A what Dr. Seuss's characters look like

  B what words Dr. Seuss made up

  C what Dr. Seuss looked like

  D what book is most popular

8 What do you learn in both passages?

  A Dr. Seuss drew cartoons.

  B Dr. Seuss wrote *Green Eggs and Ham.*

  C Sam likes green eggs and ham.

  D Some of Dr. Seuss's books are movies.

9 Give an example of a fact from passage 2. How do you know it is *not* an opinion?

_____

_____

_____

_____

10 How are the two passages alike?

_____

_____

_____

_____

PRACTICE TEST

Vocabulary
audience
backstage
cobblers
midnight
recital

Read the story. Then answer the questions.

The Shoemaker and the Elves

Once there was a shoemaker. He was very poor. He had one piece of leather left. He could make one more pair of shoes. He cut the leather for the shoes. Then he went to bed.

The next morning, the shoemaker went to his shop. There was a brand-new pair of shoes! The shoemaker did not know who had made the shoes. But they were a fine pair of shoes.

A man came into the shop. He liked the shoes very much. He even paid extra money for them. The shoemaker bought some more leather. He cut the leather. He could make two pairs of shoes. Then he went to bed.

The next morning, there were two pairs of shoes! Two people came into the shop. They bought the shoes. They paid extra money, too.

This went on day after day. Soon the shoemaker and his wife were rich! They decided to stay up late one night. They wanted to find out who was making the shoes.

midnight
12:00 at night

cobblers
people who make shoes

They hid in the shop. At midnight, two little men came in. They worked very fast. The elves made the shoes. Then they danced out of the room.

The shoemaker and his wife wanted to thank the elves. They made the elves warm clothes for winter. And they made them new shoes. They left the clothes on the table. The elves came back the next night. They put on the new clothes quickly.

The elves danced around and sang.

"What fine and dandy
boys are we!
No longer cobblers
will we be!"

Then they danced out of the room. They never came back. But the shoemaker and his wife lived happily ever after.

1. Use context clues. What are <u>elves</u>?

   A shoemakers

   B little people

   C people who wear shoes

   D cobblers

2. Where does this story take place?

   A in a bread store

   B in a toy store

   C in a hat shop

   D in a shoemaker's shop

3. When did the elves come into the shop?

   A in the morning

   B in the afternoon

   C in the evening

   D late at night

4. Which detail shows that the shoemaker is kind?

   A He is poor.

   B He wants to thank the elves.

   C People pay extra for the shoes.

   D He has a wife.

5 What can you learn only from the picture?

_____

_____

_____

_____

6 Write a summary of the story.

_____

_____

_____

_____

_____

_____

7 Who is telling this story?

   A the shoemaker

   B the elves

   C a narrator

   D the shoemaker's wife

Read the passage. Then answer the questions.

Do you like to get your hands dirty? You might like to plant your own garden. A garden can be a lot of work. But it is fun!

Decide What to Grow

First, decide what you want to grow. You need to know what the climate is where you live. Then you must learn what types of things grow best there. Ask an adult for help. Then decide what you will plant in your garden.

Glossary

Climate the weather in a certain area

Planter a box to grow plants in

All Types of Gardens

You can make a garden anywhere. Do you live in the city? Make a garden in a planter. Do you live in the country? Make a garden in the backyard.

Have fun and start growing!

There are special tools for gardening.

Send us pictures of your garden! Click on the icon here.

8 This passage is a ____.

   A magazine article

   B glossary

   C book

   D web page

9 Which text feature would you use to send a picture of your garden?

   A menu

   B icon

   C heading

   D caption

10 Look at the photograph. Read the caption. What is something you can learn just from the photograph?

_____

_____

_____

_____

Read this passage. Then answer the questions.

Sea Turtles

There are many kinds of sea turtles. They live all over the world. Some of them like very warm water. Others like cool water.

Sea turtles spend a lot of time underwater. But they have to breathe air. They come out of the water. They take a deep breath. Then they dive back under the water.

Mother sea turtles lay eggs on land. They come up on the beach at night. They slowly move across the sand. Then they dig a hole. They lay eggs in the hole. They refill the hole with sand. They smooth out the sand. It is very hard to tell where the nest is. The mothers go back to the sea.

Later, baby sea turtles come out of the eggs. They dig out of the hole. Then they go into the sea. The young sea turtles eat and grow. Sea turtles can live to be very old. Some of them can be 100 years old!

11 What does <u>refill</u> mean?

   A to fill again

   B to fill more

   C to fill before

   D to fill full

12 What is the topic of paragraph 3?

   A It is hard to find a sea turtle nest.

   B Sea turtles spend a lot of time underwater.

   C Mother sea turtles lay eggs on land.

   D Mother sea turtles come up on the beach at night.

13 Why is it hard to see the turtles' nests?

   A They are in the sand.

   B They are under the water.

   C The mothers watch over the nest.

   D The mothers smooth out the sand.

14 When do mother sea turtles lay their eggs?

   A in the morning

   B at night

   C in the winter

   D in the summer

Read the poem. Then answer the questions.

Little Boy Blue

1. Little Boy Blue,
2. Come blow your horn,
3. The sheep's in the meadow,
4. The cow's in the corn;
5. But where is the boy
6. Who looks after the sheep?
7. He's under a haystack
8. Fast asleep.
9. Will you wake him?
10. No, not I,
11. For if I do,
12. He's sure to cry.

15. What can you tell from the picture?

    A why Little Boy Blue has a horn

    B what Little Boy Blue does

    C where Little Boy Blue is sleeping

    D how many cows there are

16 Where would you *probably* find this passage?

  A in a history book

  B in a poetry book

  C in a dictionary

  D in a math book

17 Read the pairs of words from the poem. Which pair has the same vowel sound?

  A boy, who

  B blue, sure

  C cow, corn

  D sheep, asleep

Read the two passages. Then answer the questions.

Passage 1

Not Just a Game

Imagine playing a game with a ball. You try to get the ball through a hoop. But you cannot use your hands or feet! Long ago, the Maya people played a game like this. It was called pokatok. But it was much more than just a game.

The Maya people lived in parts of Mexico. They also lived in other parts of Central America.

In pokatok, two teams tried to score a goal. The players had to keep a ball in the air. It could not touch the ground. The players could not touch the ball with their hands or their feet. They could hit it with any other part of their bodies. The ball was very hard. Players had to wear pads.

Many people watched pokatok in a court like this.

The players had to get the ball through the ring.

The goal was a small ring. The ball had to go through the ring. The ring was above the players' heads. It was very hard to score a goal. The game often ended when a team scored. Sometimes the game went on for days.

The Maya did not just play pokatok for fun. Sometimes two groups of people were fighting. They would play pokatok. The winner of the game won the fight, too.

The game was part of the Maya's religion. It was very important to win the game. Sometimes the losers were killed.

Passage 2

An Old Game is New Again!

Come out this Thursday to learn a new sport! Pokatok was played thousands of years ago. The Maya people played it. It was a very important game to them. They used it to end wars. And it was part of their religion. On Thursday, we will play it just for fun!

In pokatok, you try to score a goal. You get a goal when the ball goes through a ring. You can kick the ball when it is in the air. You can hit it with your hand or your arm. You can even hit it with your head. But you cannot throw the ball. And you cannot kick it when it is on the ground.

Teams try to earn points. A team gets 7 points for a goal. Teams can also earn points for other things. Two teams play for a certain amount of time. Then the team with the most points wins!

Sign up now to be on a pokatok team! Come early to learn the basic rules. You can get some practice, too. Everyone who plays gets a T-shirt. The winning team earns a trophy! Plus everyone will have fun!

Call 555-186-9455 for more information.

See you on Thursday at Highland Park!

18 What fact do you only learn in passage 1?

  A The Maya people played pokatok.

  B Pokatok was part of their religion.

  C Pokatok players wore pads.

  D Pokatok helped end fights.

19 What is something you only learn from the pictures in passage 1?

_____

_____

_____

_____

20 Which game of pokatok could last for more than a day?

  A the game in passage 1

  B the game in passage 2

  C both games

  D neither games

21 Look at passage 1. The author says that pokatok was very important to the Maya. Which is *not* a reason that the author gives for this?

   A It was part of their religion.

   B It was used to end fights.

   C Sometimes the losers were killed.

   D It was hard to make a goal.

22 Name one way the old game of pokatok is different from the new one. Name one way it is the same.

Different _____

_____

Same _____

_____

23 What is the main idea of passage 1?

   A Pokatok was an important game to the Maya.

   B It was hard to win a game of pokatok.

   C No one plays pokatok anymore.

   D Pokatok players wore pads.

24. Look at passage 2. Which of these is an opinion?

   A You can earn different points.

   B Pokatok was played thousands of years ago.

   C But you cannot throw the ball.

   D Plus everyone will have fun!

Read two passages. Then answer the questions.

Passage 1

The Recital

Jeff took a deep breath. He sat down on the piano bench. The stage lights were bright. He could barely see the people in the audience. That was good. He tried to pretend they were not there.

He looked up at his music. He looked down at his hands. He took another deep breath. His heart was pounding like a drum. It was his first piano recital. He had to play three songs. He had practiced and practiced. But he was still nervous. He did not want to mess up.

audience
the people watching a show

recital
a time for a music or dance student to show what he has learned

Jeff's teacher smiled at him. She was waiting backstage. She nodded at him. It was time to play.

Jeff began the first song. The music filled the room. Soon he forgot about the audience. He forgot that people were listening to him. And he just played.

Suddenly he realized he was finished with his third song. He had done it! Jeff smiled. He stood up. And he took a bow.

Everyone was clapping. He knew he had messed up a couple times. But he had just kept on playing. He knew the next time he would not be as nervous.

> **backstage**
> *the area that cannot be seen by the audience*

Passage 2

The Little Engine that Could
an adaptation

Once there was a little steam engine. She was pulling a long train of cars. She puffed along happily. Then she came to a steep hill. She stopped. She looked up the hill.

"That hill is much too steep for me," she said. "I must get some help."

The little engine left the rest of the cars. She went to look for some help. Then she saw a big strong engine.

"Will you help me pull my cars up the hill?" she asked.

"I am finished working," the strong engine said. "I am going home to rest. I cannot help you."

The little engine asked two more engines. Both of them did not want to help her. The little engine chugged back to her train.

She looked up the hill again. Then she said to herself, "I think I can."

The little engine started up the hill. "I think I can, I think I can, I think I can," she said.

She moved slowly. The hill was steep. The little engine pulled and pulled. She puffed and puffed. "I think I can, I think I can, I think I can," she said.

Slowly, she moved toward the top of the hill. "I think I can, I think I can." Finally, she was there! She moved over the top of the hill! And she started down the other side.

"I thought I could, I thought I could," the little engine said. She smiled as she chugged on her way.

25 Who is telling the story in "The Recital"?
   A Jeff
   B Jeff's teacher
   C an outside narrator
   D Jeff's mom

26 What is the difference between Jeff and the little engine?
   A One is a person. One is a train.
   B One is an animal. One is a train.
   C One is a person. One is an animal.
   D One is a person. One is a car.

27 What is the same about Jeff and the little engine?

_____

_____

_____

_____

28 How can you tell that "The Little Engine that Could" is fiction?

_____

_____

_____

_____

29 Which sentence from "The Recital" uses language playfully?

  A The stage lights were bright.

  B His heart was pounding like a drum.

  C The music filled the room.

  D Everyone was clapping.

30 What lesson can you learn from these two stories?

_____

_____

_____

_____

GLOSSARY

A
Antonyms	words with an opposite meaning
Argument	not thinking the same about something
Audience	the people watching a show

B
Backstage	the area that cannot be seen by the audience
Burrow	a hole where an animal lives

C
Cast	to throw a fishing line into the water
Castles	large homes for kings and queens, like palaces
Chores	work that needs to be done
Chuckled	laughed
Coach	a beautiful wagon to ride in, pulled by horses
Cobblers	people who make shoes
Collect	to gather a group of something
Comet	an object from space with a long tail
Community	a group of people living together

	Confused	not sure
	Controls	things used to move an object where you want it to go
D	**Dwarf**	small
E	**Enemy**	the people you are against
	Engine	something that makes a moving object run
	Exaggerate	to stretch the truth
	Exercise	moving your body
	Explore	to look at and discover
	Extinct	when there are no more of a certain animal alive
F	**Fact**	a statement or information that can be proven
	Famous	well-known
	Frightened	scared
H	**Harvest**	to pick vegetables that are ripe
	Honor	to show that someone is special

 **Key words**   list of important words in a text

 **Languages**   ways of speaking

 **Mangrove**   a tree that grows in some swamps

Metaphor   type of figurative language that compares two unlike things but does not use *like* or *as*

Midnight   12:00 at night

Moisture   wetness

 **Nutrition**   things that animals and people need to stay healthy

Observe   to watch something so you can learn about it

Office   a room where someone does his work

Opinion   something that someone believes or thinks

Outwit   to trick, to be smarter than someone

P

Passages	hallways
Point of view	who is telling the story
Politics	work in the government
Porridge	oatmeal
Prefix	part of a word added to the beginning of another word that changes the meaning of the word
President	the head of the United States
Products	things that are made
Protect	to keep safe
Published	to be printed and sold
Pyramids	large buildings with four walls that are shaped like triangles

R

Recital	a time for a music or dance student to show what he has learned
Reel	to bring a fish on a line in from the water
Requirement	something that is needed
Rescue	to save
Rhyme	when words have the same ending sounds
Roam	to travel around

S

Scent	a smell
Schedule	something that tells time and order of things that are happening
Simile	type of figurative language that compares two unlike things using *as* or *like*
Stalls	places in a barn where animals are kept
Sternly	in a firm way
Stilts	things to walk on to make you taller
Stories	the floors in a building
Suffix	part of a word added to the end of another word that changes the meaning of the word
Swamp	land that is wet and often covered in water
Synonyms	words that have a similar meaning

 **Traffic**   cars and trucks on roads

Trapper   a person who catches wild animals with traps

Treasures   things that are worth a lot

Triangular   in the shape of a triangle

 **Wrestled**   to fight something to the ground